MARKING 20 YEARS

KEMPER MUSEUM of CONTEMPORARY ART

KEMPER MUSEUM *of*

MARKING 20 YEARS

CONTEMPORARY ART

Kansas City, Missouri

Contents

Foreword

New ideas take shape. Skylines morph dramatically. Whole cities transform. Great museums stand the test of time and contribute to the cultural landscape, serving as both a sanctuary for the preservation of culture and an impetus for change.

Since 1994, the Kemper Museum of Contemporary Art has enjoyed the great privilege of bringing current and compelling visual art to Kansas City and presenting it, free, to our regional audience. Our mission to nurture, challenge, and inspire the community is as strong today as it was when my mother and father opened the doors of the Kemper Museum twenty years ago. My parents, Bebe and Crosby Kemper, harnessed their shared passion for art to create a very special museum with the understanding that contemporary art can be synonymous with growth when it comes to strengthening a city and invigorating its people.

The Kemper Museum has played an important role in my personal life—like that of a trusted mentor, inspiring me from age seventeen. I have been both challenged and moved by countless exhibitions and artists, singular works of art, lectures, programs, conversations, and of course the artful creations plated at Café Sebastienne. My own creative path was encouraged by prolific artists in our Permanent Collection who entrusted me to make films about their lives and/or life's work. My husband, Gary, and I hold dear memories of being married in the main gallery, surrounded by the sumptuous and delectable canvases of Wayne Thiebaud's cakes and pies, and now I delight in seeing our children, Benjamin and Georgia, discover the power of a relationship with art. It was also fitting that my father's memorial reception was held in our Museum atrium. The gathering proved to be a remarkable tribute to how much the Kemper Museum has enriched so many lives.

Today I have the honor of looking toward the next twenty years in the life of the Kemper Museum. As Chairman of the Board of Trustees, I am ever mindful of the importance of continuing our mission to provide high-quality art, education, and community-minded experiences, as well as collaborating in new ways with other local art-loving institutions and individuals. My goals are to honor the legacy of my parents while attracting new and diverse audiences, providing access to even more cutting-edge art, and developing additional strategic alliances in our community. We have just launched our No Boundaries teen initiative art program for students ages thirteen to fifteen. It is exciting to think how the Museum will work to nurture and encourage young artists from all over the metro!

Of course, the Kemper Museum could not have thrived these past twenty years without the commitment of our talented and knowledgeable staff and selfless, energized docents, interns, and volunteers. A huge debt of gratitude is owed to the steadfast members of the Board of Trustees who have contributed to the Museum's success far longer than I have, and to our devoted Board of Directors. In addition, the generous benefactors who have made financial gifts

Mary Kemper Wolf

or gifts of art—those who are acknowledged within these pages and all those who have come before them—have been an essential ingredient in our success. Only with this combined dedication and the unwavering support of our members and community has the Kemper Museum been able to make an impactful contribution to our beloved city and to the larger art world. I look forward to the amazing art and exploration that the Kemper Museum of Contemporary Art will share with our community for many years to come.

Mary Kemper Wolf
Chairman, Board of Trustees
Kemper Museum of Contemporary Art

Bringing Art to Life:
The Kemper Museum at 20

The Kemper Museum with Louise Bourgeois's *Spider* (1996)

The pendulum swing of aesthetic language means that certain words will move in and out of style. The term "Beauty" is certainly one of those. At the Kemper Museum of Contemporary Art, we are inspired by the words of our co-founder, R. Crosby Kemper Jr. (1927–2014): "My joy is to be surrounded by beauty, and what is more beautiful than great art?" We strive to have the beauty—whether elegant or awkward, poetic or prosaic, seemingly obvious or ultimately inscrutable—of modern and contemporary art draw our visitors into a dialogue of the life well lived. We bring art to life.

This sense of forward momentum, of being on the leading edge of what makes a great museum, is palpably present in the twenty-year history of the Kemper Museum of Contemporary Art. Crosby, as he was familiarly known, set the Museum on an extraordinary course when he and his wife, Mary "Bebe" Stripp Kemper, donated the first 320 works that are the conceptual core of the Museum's Permanent Collection. That original gift, made in 1993, included an exceptional selection of art in diverse styles, traditions, and media. Paintings by Stuart Davis, Janet Fish, Grace Hartigan, Philip Pearlstein, and Wayne Thiebaud, and sculpture by Deborah Butterfield, Nancy Graves, Duane Hanson, Bruce Nauman, and Frank Stella only begin to suggest the eye

The Kemper Museum with Tom Otterness's *Crying Giant* (2002)

for quality and significance that these works represent. A focus on excellence, knowledge of the artist, and place of the work in the history of both the artist's career and the history of the art of our time have been the guiding principles of building the Museum's Collection, which now includes more than 1,200 works of art.

We strive to find a place in the lives of not only occasional visitors to the Kemper Museum, but also our neighbors, with whom we share a commitment to civic engagement and the advancement of Kansas City. The Museum's dramatic Gunnar Birkerts-designed structure, which opened to the public in 1994, became part of a larger cultural campus that includes the Kansas City Art Institute and the Nelson-Atkins Museum of Art, both within easy walking distance. The grounds of the Kemper Museum boast significant sculptures that have become civic icons that engage visitors even before they walk under the porte cochere and enter the light-filled, welcoming atrium. *Spider* (1996) by Louise Bourgeois and *Crying Giant* (2002) by Tom Otterness are subjects for "photo ops" that visitors capture as a memory of a moment of challenge and delight. The renovation of a nearby historic home in the mid-2000s and its subsequent renaming as "Kemper East" gave administrative offices a much-needed expansion and offered an additional, more intimate venue for changing exhibitions of works from the Permanent Collection. Over the past few years, the work on view at Kemper East has enhanced visitors' connection to the changing exhibitions in the Museum's Charlotte Crosby Kemper Gallery (familiarly known as "the main gallery"). The graceful Kemper East, in its historic neighborhood setting, is given dramatic counterpoint by the siting of Jules Olitski's sculpture *Eos the Titan* (2006), a vibrant orange slice of a cement mixer transformed through the artist's sensibility.

Kemper East with Jules Olitski's *Eos the Titan* (2006)

The Kemper Museum's role as not only an important cultural, but also an active civic partner to Kansas City and the region is evidenced by the "numbers," but also by the intangible experiences of engagement with art. Our attendance figures (millions of visitors since opening in 1994) support an understanding that cultural tourism is significant to the economy of the region. Closer to home, our docent-led school tours, public programs for children and adults, summer camps, and teen-

Childe Hassam, *Nude, Appledore, Isle of Shoals* (1913)

focused programs (never at any cost to the participants) expand and deepen our mission-driven commitment to interpretation and education.

While 2014 marks twenty years of collecting, caring for, and exhibiting significant modern and contemporary art, the Collection itself spans one hundred years of artistic creation. Among the earliest works in the Collection, *Nude, Appledore, Isle of Shoals* by Childe Hassam, dates from 1913. Hassam's practice exemplifies the shift of the epicenter of the art world from Paris to New York. As a conceptual bridge from the twentieth to the twenty-first century, the Kemper Museum's Permanent Collection traces the history of art from a European to an American power base and now to a global arena where artists are often citizens of the world, claiming neither one country nor even a continent as point of origin or inspiration. As the twenty-first century moved into its second decade, the Collection increasingly reflected this global reality with the addition of sculptural installations *Go Go Green Compression: Mix More Media!* (2010) and *Go Go Gone* (2011) by the Afro-Caribbean artist Nicole Awai; a large-scale color photograph, *Les Femmes du Maroc: La Grande Odalisque* (2008), by the Moroccan artist Lalla Essaydi; and a painting by Susanne Kühn, *Regina arbeitet (Regina Working)* (2009). Kühn was born behind the Berlin Wall, only experiencing a global perspective at age twenty when, in 1989, the wall came crashing down.

Raising the Kemper Museum's national profile goes hand-in-hand with our contribution to the field of art history through scholarship, exhibitions, and publications. During the first decade, the Museum organized and toured significant exhibitions including *Ken Aptekar: Painting Between the Lines, 1990–2000* (2001) and *Frederick J. Brown: Portraits in Jazz, Blues, and Other Icons* (2002) which connected the paintings in the Charlotte Crosby Kemper Gallery to *The History of Art*, Brown's extraordinary installation of 110 interlocking canvases on permanent view in the Museum's renowned Café Sebastienne. More recently, the Kemper Museum organized and premiered *Revelation: Major Paintings by Jules Olitski* (2011) with an accompanying monographic catalogue. *Revelation* then traveled to the Museum of Fine Arts, Houston, Texas; the Toledo Museum of Art, Ohio; the

David Bates: The Katrina Paintings (2010), installation view

American University Museum at the Katzen Arts Center, Washington, D.C.; and finally the Baker Museum of Art, Naples, Florida, where it closed in 2013. Other recent exhibitions, with accompanying publications, that premiered at the Kemper and then traveled to museums across the United States include *Dan Christensen: Forty Years of Painting* (2009); *David Bates: The Katrina Paintings* (2010); and *Lois Dodd: Catching the Light* (2012).

As the Kemper Museum entered its second decade, two projects reflected a bold leap into the urban arena. The first was a series of public art commissions made possible through a public-private alliance with DST Systems, Inc., and initiated by then-Museum Director Rachael Blackburn Cozad. Three sculptures—*Mesteño (Mustang)* (1997–2001) by Luis Jimenez; *Putto 2x2x4* (2005) by Michael Rees; and *Descent of Civilization (Bison Memorial)* (2010) by Marc Swanson—are evidence that art can both engage and challenge a community. Provocatively sited in downtown Kansas City, Missouri, each commission was several years in the planning and creation, offering the

Ride or Die (2013–14), exterior view at Kemper at the Crossroads

artists an opportunity to find important historic and contemporaneous connections to Kansas City's original downtown where workers in the banking, finance, hospitality, and tech sectors pass by each day.

Jeff Shore and Jon Fisher: Reel to Reel (2008–9), installation view

Another commitment to a more vivid public presence in the community came in 2008 with the purchase of a building at 19th and Baltimore Streets in the Crossroads district of Kansas City. Affectionately called "Kemper at the Crossroads," this venue offered a location for new ideas, exhibitions, and programs, joining forces with a district already known for galleries, restaurants, small independent businesses, and live/work spaces. "Our new front door is the street!" is a catchphrase for this stunning multi-gallery space that features floor-to-ceiling windows for spectacular viewing of the exhibitions both day and night. While we launched exhibition programming in this new space in 2008, major renovations began in earnest in 2010 (and are still ongoing as of early 2014). Exhibitions at Kemper at the Crossroads have featured exciting presentations of works by artists on the leading edge of impressive careers. The sound and video installation *Jeff Shore and Jon Fisher: Reel to Reel* (2008–9) inaugurated the Crossroads exhibitions, followed by *Jaimie Warren: You Are So Beautiful in the Face* (2009), the first solo museum exhibition for this recent graduate of the Kansas City Art Institute. Dramatic gallery installations by artists who fuse fine art and fine craft have included *When the Women Sing* (2010) by Argentinian-born fiber artist Ana Maria Hernando, in which a "river" of crocheted petticoats delighted

Docent-led tour of *The Big Reveal* (2011–12)

visitors; Jeanne Quinn's glowing *Ceramic In(ter)ventions* (2011) which lit up the night; and *Here's Your Hat, What's Your Hurry?* (2012) by Eric Fertman, a sculptor who creates humorous sculptures and drawings in which the elegance of Constantin Brancusi meets the comic forms of Philip Guston. These exhibitions and many more have engaged new, diverse audiences during the always-vibrant First Fridays at the Crossroads.

The Kemper Museum's enviable growth in its second decade is reflected in the expansion from one location to three. Rotating exhibitions and accompanying public programs encourage visitors to not only engage with modern and contemporary art but also with the artists of our time. Our support of emerging and midcareer artists makes us a leader in the field, with many artists having their first major, solo, or U.S. exhibition at the Kemper Museum. Providing access to living artists is the norm at the Kemper Museum and is an invaluable experience for Museum visitors and the community at large. Every exhibition at both the Kemper Museum and Kemper at the Crossroads features

Kemper Street Museum at the Plaza Art Fair

organized complementary public programs where dialogue is central, whether a question and answer between the curator and artist, an artist talk with images from past (and sometimes still-in-progress) art, or a workshop such as the one where June Ahrens (*Acquisitions in Context: June Ahrens* [2011]) spent a day with participants making memory jars in recognition of the tenth anniversary of 9/11. The Double Visions program series pairs experts in fields other than visual art (such as cartography, Victorian hair braiding, or street theater) with an artist for an always-lively dialogue.

Each year, as part of the three-day Plaza Art Fair, the Kemper Street Museum creates fun, interactive activities for children based on the major exhibition on view at the Museum.

Visitors of all ages and abilities have enjoyed a wide range of accessible public programs including storytelling, Art(full) bags with self-guided activities to use in the galleries, a new band trying out their sound, and luminous nighttime

Students from the Kemper Museum's No Boundaries teen art initiative touring *Dressed Up* (2013–14)

mapping of the grounds of the Museum. We are particularly proud of community partnerships such as ArtReach, where with the support of staff from the University of Kansas Medical Center, children of all abilities create art together in the galleries. Or when a nutritionist discusses healthy eating in the Museum atrium while local green grocers

The Gao Brothers with *Mao's Guilt* (2009), in *Gao Brothers: Grandeur and Catharsis* (2010–11)

showcase free produce in a cart on the Museum grounds. This sort of inventive, unexpected programming keeps the Museum relevant and meaningful to our varied audiences. And reaching beyond our three physical locations, podcasts of interviews with visiting artists have further expanded the reach of their voices and Museum programming, through a partnership with public radio station KCUR.

The Kemper Museum has in a short twenty years become one of the signature cultural organizations in the region. The Museum has consistently made bold and forward-thinking decisions both with additions to the Permanent Collection and with a record of significant scholarship in the organizing of important exhibitions and the creation of publications. In 2010 the Museum stretched internationally to be the only museum in the United States to feature a solo exhibition of works by the Gao Brothers. These brothers, who have suffered from the echoes of Mao's China, traveled to Kansas City from Beijing for the opening of their show, *Gao Brothers: Grandeur and Catharsis*. The near-frenzy of visitors, thrilled to talk with and have their photos taken with these art world celebrities, shared the experience globally on Facebook. After the Gaos' twenty-foot-high, stainless steel sculpture, *Miss Mao Trying to Poise Herself at the Top of Lenin's Head* (2009), was installed on the grounds of the Museum, the students at the nearby Kansas City Art Institute quickly nicknamed it "the Big Shiny" and left notes and books at its base. This sort of activated connection to the community is what living artists can create.

The Permanent Collection is the base upon which our education mission and programming are founded and from which they spring. Whether acquiring *Untitled #1336 (Scalupino Nu Shu)* (2009–10), a sculpture by Petah Coyne that incorporates a full-grown apple tree festooned with taxidermied peacocks and pheasants, or adding Richard Mosse's mesmerizing *Men of Good Fortune* (2011), a large-scale photograph that used U.S. military heat-seeking film to create a psychedelic pink landscape of the Congo, beauty and drama are the first calling cards that move us as viewers toward the poetics, meaning, and challenges of contemporary art. The Museum offers visitors opportunities for dialogue with artists and docents, with curators and education staff, and perhaps most importantly

A Museum docent leading a discussion of Trenton Doyle Hancock's series *The Year*, in *Dressed Up* (2013–14)

with the work of art itself in an environment that is open, light filled, and engaging.

Art can and does change lives. Our dedicated and experienced volunteer docents offer engaging tours to students, intergenerational groups, and visitors from across the United States. Every visitor, at whatever age and from whatever geographic location, comes to the Museum with an active imagination and the desire to experience, learn, and engage. All are open to the power of art to inspire and to the

myriad ways that the Kemper Museum of Contemporary Art brings art to life. I am looking forward in a shared belief with our Trustees, staff, and visitors that the next twenty years will be filled with great meaning and promise.

Barbara O'Brien
Executive Director
Kemper Museum of Contemporary Art

Barbara O'Brien

KEMPER MUSEUM

KEMPER EAST

KEMPER AT THE CROSSROADS

Selections from the Permanent Collection

Magdalena **Abakanowicz**

Sage Y, 1988
burlap, resin, steel
57½ x 23 x 33 inches
Bebe and Crosby Kemper Collection
Museum purchase, Enid and Crosby Kemper and William T. Kemper
Acquisition Fund, 2005.2a–b

Josef **Albers**

I-SF: SK-ED, 1970–71
screen print, edition 65/100
13¾ x 13¾ inches
Bebe and Crosby Kemper Collection
Gift of Mr. and Mrs. R. Crosby Kemper Jr., 1995.1

Jose **Alvarez** (D.O.P.A.)

Forever Radiant, 2009
feathers, porcupine quills, crystals, collage on
inkjet print on archival paper mounted on board
24 x 19 inches
Bebe and Crosby Kemper Collection
Museum purchase made possible by a gift from
the R. C. Kemper Charitable Trust, 2010.15

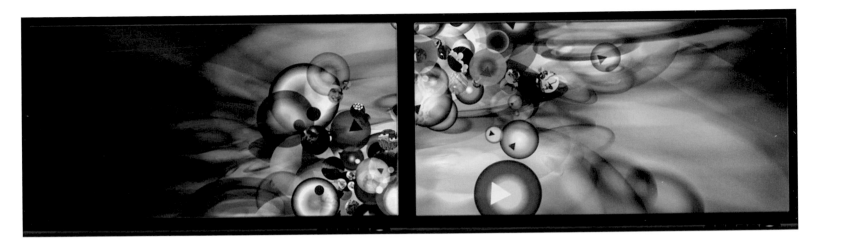

Barry **Anderson**

Janus (2), 2011
two-channel HD video animation, edition 1/5
27¼ x 84¾ inches, 4:00 min. loop
Bebe and Crosby Kemper Collection
Museum purchase made possible by a gift from the
R. C. Kemper Charitable Trust, 2011.1a–b

Pigeon, 2001
single-channel video with stereo sound, edition 2/5
dimensions variable, 7:37 min. loop
Gift of the artist, 2011.2

Polly **Apfelbaum**

Split, 1998
synthetic velvet and fabric dye
dimensions variable
Bebe and Crosby Kemper Collection
Museum purchase, Enid and Crosby Kemper and
William T. Kemper Acquisition Fund, 2004.7a–h

Alexander **Archipenko**

Femme Assise, 1912
bronze, edition 8/12
15½ x 10 x 8 inches
Bebe and Crosby Kemper Collection
Museum purchase, Enid and Crosby Kemper and
William T. Kemper Acquisition Fund, 2005.27

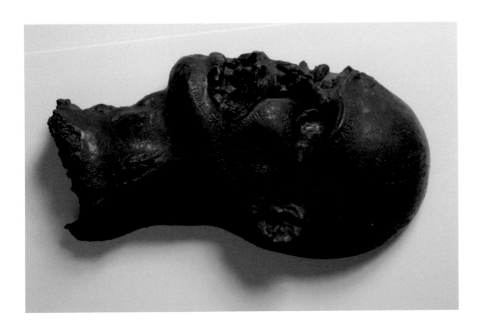

Robert **Arneson**

Nuclear Head #3, 1983
glazed stoneware
13 x 23 x 5½ inches
Gift of Mr. and Mrs. Arthur J. Kase
and Joanne and Lee Lyon, 2005.38

Nicole **Awai**

Go Go Gone, 2011
acrylic, polyurethane resin, nail polish,
graphite on wood and foam
72 x 60 x 48 inches
Gift of the Vilcek Foundation, 2012.8.2a–w

Go Go Green Compression: Mix More Media!, 2010
graphite, acrylic, nail polish on paper
38 x 50 inches
Gift of the Vilcek Foundation, 2012.8.1

Francis **Bacon**

Seated Figure 1977, 1992
etching and aquatint on paper, edition 57/90
52⅜ x 38⅝ inches
Bebe and Crosby Kemper Collection
Gift of the R. C. Kemper Charitable Trust, 2012.17

David **Bates**

The Storm, 2006–07
oil on canvas, triptych
60 x 254 inches (overall), 60 x 84 inches (left),
60 x 86 inches (center), 60 x 84 inches (right)
Bebe and Crosby Kemper Collection
Museum purchase made possible by gifts from
the Enid and Crosby Kemper Foundation and
the R. C. Kemper Charitable Trust, 2010.19a–c

(detail)

Study for Flood Water, 2006
watercolor on paper
13¾ x 11 inches
Gift of Jan Lee Bates and the artist, 2010.23.6

Romare **Bearden**

Family, 1971
paint, photographs, fabric, paper on board
22½ x 25¾ inches
Bebe and Crosby Kemper Collection
Gift of the William T. Kemper Charitable Trust,
UMB Bank, n.a., Trustee, 1999.13

Evening Lamp, 1986
watercolor and collage on board
21¾ x 18¾ inches
Museum purchase made possible by a gift from
the Kearney Wornall Foundation, UMB Bank, n.a., Trustee, 2011.3

Thomas Hart **Benton**

Desert Artist, 1962
oil on canvas
40 x 32 inches
Bebe and Crosby Kemper Collection
Gift of Mr. and Mrs. R. Crosby Kemper Jr., 2000.2

Robin **Bernat**

American Pastoral, 2001
three-channel video projection, edition of 20
original music written and produced by Railroad Earth Studio,
Neil Fried and Clark Vreeland, with the exception of *Daniel's
Song*, written by Robin Bernat
dimensions variable, 45:00 min. loop
Gift of the artist, 2003.7a–c

Ed **Blackburn**

Abstract Marlon, 2012
archival digital print, edition 1/3
22 x 17 inches
Gift of Linda and Ed Blackburn in honor of the 20th Anniversary
of the Kemper Museum of Contemporary Art, 2013.8

Blue Car, 2012
archival digital print, edition 1/3
22 x 17 inches
Gift of Linda and Ed Blackburn in honor of the 20th Anniversary
of the Kemper Museum of Contemporary Art, 2013.9

Julie **Blackmon**

Gum, 2005
pigment print, edition 25/25
24 x 24½ inches
Bebe and Crosby Kemper Collection
Gift of the R. C. Kemper Charitable Trust, 2008.11

Stolen Kiss, 2005
pigment print, edition 6/25
24 x 24½ inches
Bebe and Crosby Kemper Collection
Gift of the R. C. Kemper Charitable Trust, 2008.9

Christian **Boltanski**

20 Dead Swiss, 1990
photographs, glass, tape, metal lamps, wire
124 x 80½ x 13½ inches
Gift of Museum Without Walls, Kansas City, Missouri,
and the Sosland Family, 1997.17

Chakaia **Booker**

El Gato, 2001
rubber tire and wood
48 x 42 x 42 inches
Bebe and Crosby Kemper Collection
Museum purchase, Enid and Crosby Kemper and William T. Kemper
Acquisition Fund, 2004.12

Fernando **Botero**

La Pudeur, 1981
bronze, edition 6/6
60 x 24 x 21 inches
Bebe and Crosby Kemper Collection
Gift of Mr. and Mrs. R. Crosby Kemper Jr., 1998.15

Louise **Bourgeois**

Spider, 1996, cast 1997
bronze, edition 3/6
133 x 263 x 249 inches
Bebe and Crosby Kemper Collection
Gift of the William T. Kemper Charitable
Trust, UMB Bank, n.a., Trustee, 1997.7.2

Christopher **Brown**

Elm Street, 1995
oil on linen
88 x 95 inches
Gift of the E. Kemper Carter and
Anna Curry Carter Community Memorial Trust,
UMB Bank, n.a., Trustee, 1996.3

Continental II, 1995/2013
oil on linen
20 x 20 inches
Gift of Christopher Brown and John Berggruen
Gallery in honor of the 20th Anniversary of the
Kemper Museum of Contemporary Art, 2013.20

Reach, 1994
oil on linen
20 x 20 inches
Bebe and Crosby Kemper Collection
Gift of Mr. and Mrs. R. Crosby Kemper Jr., 2005.33

41

Frederick James **Brown**

Dexter Gordon, 2005
mixed media on canvas on wood panel
60⅛ x 50⅛ inches
Bebe and Crosby Kemper Collection
Gift of the Enid and Crosby Kemper Foundation, 2008.22

Johnnie Hodges, 2005
mixed media on canvas on wood panel
60⅛ x 50⅛ inches
Bebe and Crosby Kemper Collection
Gift of the Enid and Crosby Kemper Foundation, 2008.23

The History of Art (installation view), 1994/2001
oil and acrylic on canvas
site-specific commission of 110 shaped, interlocking canvases
dimensions variable
Bebe and Crosby Kemper Collection
Gift of the William T. Kemper Charitable Trust, UMB Bank, n.a., Trustee,
1999.20.1–108, 2001.1.1–2

43

Deborah **Butterfield**

Ahulani, 1991
bronze
53 x 119 x 36 inches
Bebe and Crosby Kemper Collection
Gift of the William T. Kemper Charitable Trust,
UMB Bank, n.a., Trustee, 1995.12

Ingrid **Calame**

#112 Working Drawing, 2002
colored pencil on trace Mylar
88 x 88 inches
Bebe and Crosby Kemper Collection
Museum purchase made possible by a gift from
the R. C. Kemper Charitable Trust, 2012.9

Harry **Callahan**

Eleanor, Indiana, 1948
gelatin silver print
4½ x 4½ inches
Gift of Susan and Peter MacGill, Pace/MacGill Gallery,
New York, 1995.91

Bob Fine, 1952
gelatin silver print
9¾ x 7¾ inches
Bebe and Crosby Kemper Collection
Gift of the Enid and Crosby Kemper Foundation, 1995.13

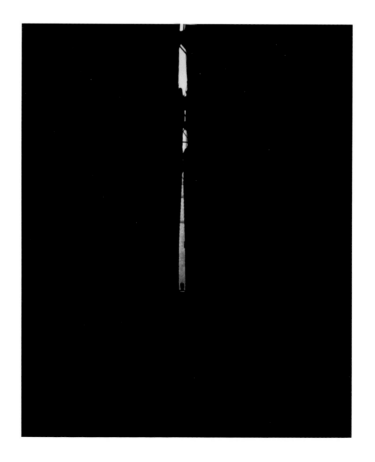

Suzanne **Caporael**

Jade Bay, North Sea, Germany, 2003
from the *Salt Marsh Suite*
lithograph with hand painting, pencil, chine collé
on kozo paper, edition 6/30
19¼ x 13⅛ inches
Bebe and Crosby Kemper Collection
Museum purchase made possible by a gift from
the R. C. Kemper Charitable Trust, 2010.2.3

Sapelo Island Creek, Georgia, 2003
from the *Salt Marsh Suite*
lithograph with hand painting, pencil, chine collé
on kozo paper, edition 6/30
19¼ x 13⅛ inches
Bebe and Crosby Kemper Collection
Museum purchase made possible by a gift from
the R. C. Kemper Charitable Trust, 2010.2.5

Squeak **Carnwath**

Recorded Life, 2006
cotton tapestry, edition 1/8
81 x 72 inches
Bebe and Crosby Kemper Collection
Museum purchase, Enid and Crosby Kemper and
William T. Kemper Acquisition Fund, 2006.16

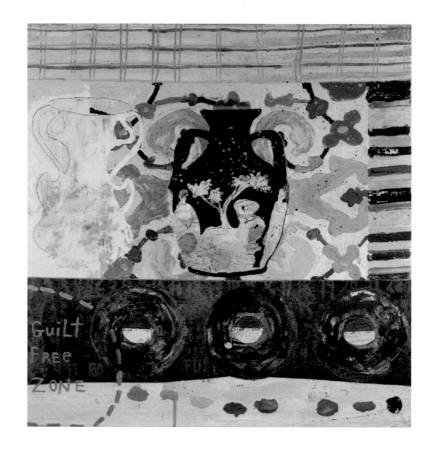

Brendan **Cass**

Capri, 2009
acrylic on canvas
78 x 132 inches
Bebe and Crosby Kemper Collection
Museum purchase made possible by a gift from the William
T. Kemper Charitable Trust, UMB Bank, n.a., Trustee, 2012.3

John **Chamberlain**

Apparentlyoffspring, 1992
acrylic on steel
48 x 70 x 56 inches
Bebe and Crosby Kemper Collection
Gift of the Enid and Crosby Kemper Foundation, 2012.14

Dale **Chihuly**

Palazzo di Loredana Balboni (detail), 1996
glass
west wall (shown): 116 x 62 x 32 inches
east wall: 112 x 64 x 32 inches
Gift of the artist, 1996.33

Kemper Museum of Contemporary Art Persian Wall, 1996
glass
60 x 208 x 18 inches
Gift of the artist, 1996.34

Campiello del Remer, 1996
crystal
144 x 65 x 60 inches
Gift of the artist, 1996.32

Dan **Christensen**

Lisa's Red, 1971
enamel, acrylic, Japan Color on canvas
102 x 88 inches
Bebe and Crosby Kemper Collection
Gift of the Enid and Crosby Kemper Foundation, 1995.15

Coaxed Red, 1994
acrylic on canvas
40½ x 29½ inches
Gift of Robert L. Bloch, 2001.18

Jacob **Collins**

Richard, 2011
oil on canvas
26¼ x 26 inches
Bebe and Crosby Kemper Collection
Gift of the R. C. Kemper Charitable Trust, 2012.18

Joseph **Cornell**

La Gaîté (2), 1965
paper collage on board
17½ x 13½ inches
Bebe and Crosby Kemper Collection
Gift of the William T. Kemper Charitable Trust,
UMB Bank, n.a., Trustee, 2012.21

Untitled #1336 (Scalapino Nu Shu), 2009–10
apple tree, taxidermy Black Melanistic Pheasants, taxidermy
Blue India Peacocks, taxidermy Black-Shouldered Peacocks,
taxidermy Spaulding Peacocks, black sand from pig iron casting,
Acrylex 234, black paint, cement, chicken-wire fencing, wood,
gravel, sisal, staging rope, cotton rope, insulated foam sealant,
pipe, epoxy, threaded rod, wire, screws, jaw-to-jaw swivels
158 x 264 x 288 inches
Bebe and Crosby Kemper Collection
Museum purchase made possible by a gift from the
R. C. Kemper Charitable Trust, 2011.7a–aaw

54   (detail)

Untitled #827 (Three Tiered Chandelier), 1996
wax, pigment, ribbons, candles, artificial birds and
flowers, satin, steel
216 x 62 x 63 inches
Bebe and Crosby Kemper Collection
Museum purchase, Enid and Crosby Kemper and
William T. Kemper Acquisition Fund, 2005.25a–r

(detail)

Willem **de Kooning**

Untitled, 1977
oil, enamel, charcoal on canvas
60 x 48 inches
Promised gift of the William T. Kemper Charitable Trust, UMB Bank, n.a., Trustee, L1999.2

Untitled (Woman), 1971
mixed media on newsprint on board
45¼ x 29¼ inches
Bebe and Crosby Kemper Collection
Gift of the Enid and Crosby Kemper Foundation, 1995.23

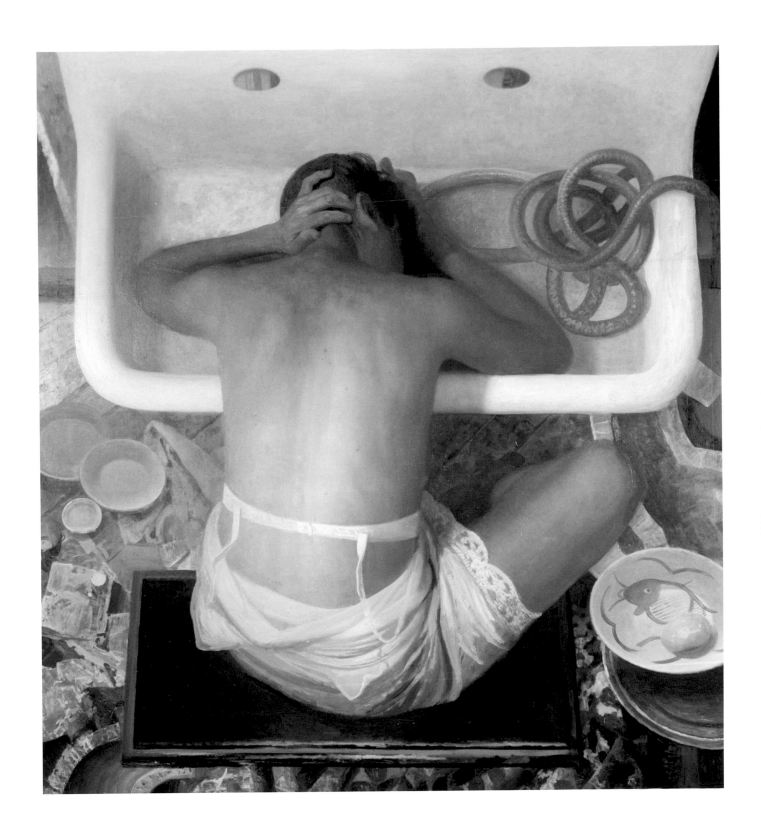

Vincent **Desiderio**

Soaking, 2005
oil on linen
78½ x 71½ inches
Bebe and Crosby Kemper Collection
Museum purchase, Enid and Crosby Kemper and
William T. Kemper Acquisition Fund, 2005.20

Lois **Dodd**

Men's Shelter, April, 1968
oil on linen
48⅜ x 40½ inches
Bebe and Crosby Kemper Collection
Museum purchase made possible by a gift from the William T. Kemper
Charitable Trust, UMB Bank, n.a., Trustee, 2012.2

The Derrick, 1930
oil on canvas
30⅛ x 40⅛ inches
Bebe and Crosby Kemper Collection
Gift of the William T. Kemper Charitable Trust, UMB Bank, n.a.,
Trustee, and the Enid and Crosby Kemper Foundation, 2000.4

Arthur **Dove**

October, 1935
oil on canvas
14 x 70 inches
Bebe and Crosby Kemper Collection
Gift of the R. C. Kemper Charitable Trust, 1996.16

Angela **Dufresne**

*The lost fishing village of Diderot, Boucher, and Lorraine
or the movie set of pioneer legacy*, 2009
oil on canvas
72 x 90 inches
Gift of the American Academy of Arts and Letters, New York:
Hassam, Speicher, Betts and Symons funds, 2011, 2011.9

Michael **Eastman**

Isabella's Two Chairs, 2000
chromogenic color print
53¾ x 39¾ inches
Bebe and Crosby Kemper Collection
Museum purchase, Enid and Crosby Kemper
and William T. Kemper Acquisition Fund, 2003.20

Lalla **Essaydi**

Les Femmes du Maroc: La Grande Odalisque, 2008
chromogenic color print on aluminum, edition 8/10
48 x 58 inches
Bebe and Crosby Kemper Collection
Museum purchase made possible by a gift from the
R. C. Kemper Charitable Trust, 2011.10

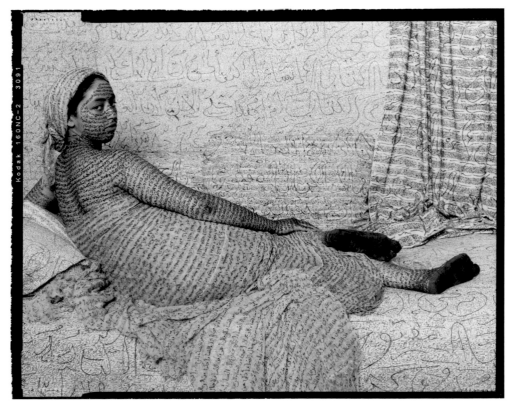

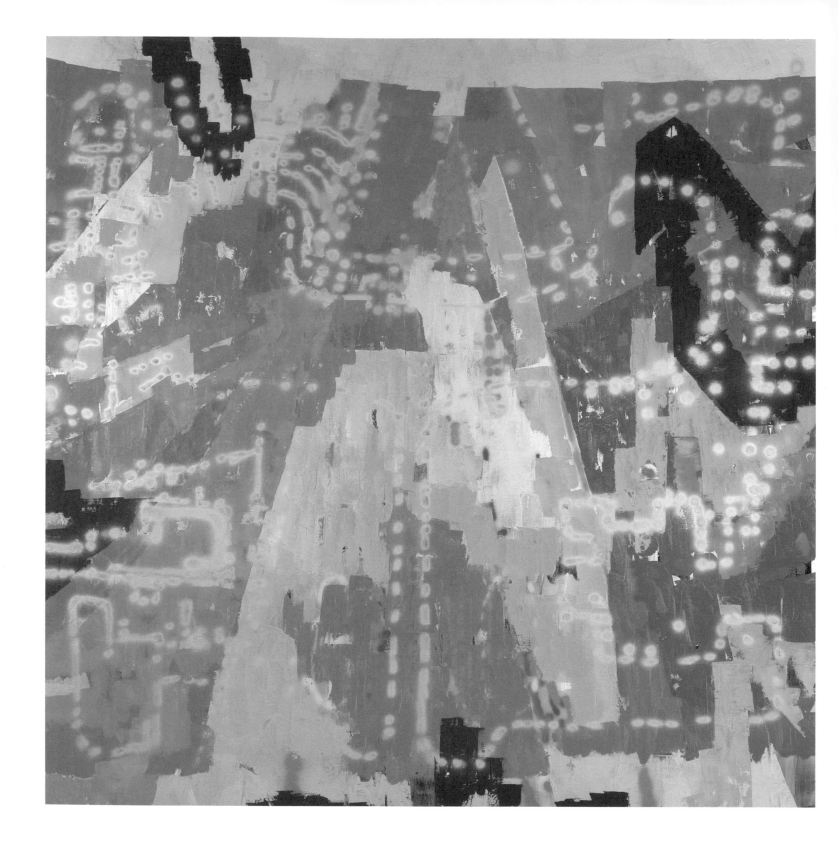

Keltie **Ferris**

The Wrestler, 2009
oil and acrylic on canvas
80 x 80 inches
Bebe and Crosby Kemper Collection
Museum purchase made possible by a gift from
the R. C. Kemper Charitable Trust, 2009.16

Sam **Francis**

Untitled, 1979
watercolor on paper
8 x 6 inches
Gift of the Sam Francis Foundation, 2013.3

Untitled, 1980
acrylic on paper
16 x 9 inches
Gift of the Sam Francis Foundation, 2013.4

Helen **Frankenthaler**

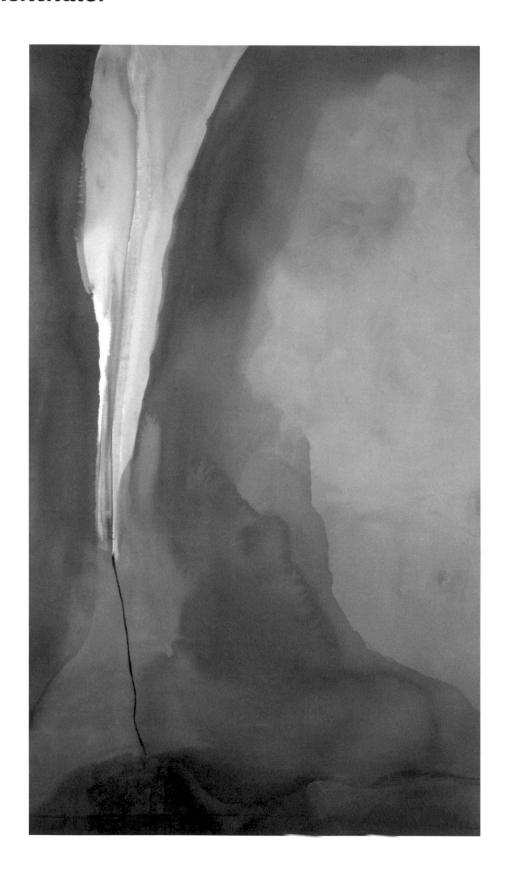

Coral Wedge, 1972
acrylic on canvas
81½ x 46½ inches
Bebe and Crosby Kemper Collection
Gift of the Enid and Crosby Kemper Foundation, 1995.32

Midnight Shore, 2002
acrylic on canvas
55¾ x 35½ inches
Bebe and Crosby Kemper Collection
Museum purchase made possible by a gift from
the R. C. Kemper Charitable Trust, 2004.18

Warming Trend, 2002
acrylic on canvas
74¾ x 84½ inches
Bebe and Crosby Kemper Collection
Gift of the William T. Kemper Charitable Trust,
UMB Bank, n.a., Trustee, 2011.32

Gajin **Fujita**

Ride or Die, 2005
spray paint, paint marker, paint stick,
gold and white gold leaf on wood panels
84 x 132½ inches
Bebe and Crosby Kemper Collection
Museum purchase, Enid and Crosby Kemper and
William T. Kemper Acquisition Fund, 2005.39a–c

Hope **Gangloff**

Vera, 2013
acrylic on canvas
81 x 54 inches
Museum purchase made possible by
a gift from Paul Uhlmann Jr., 2013.2

Gao Brothers

Miss Mao, 2006
painted fiberglass, edition 8/8
82 x 50 x 48 inches
Bebe and Crosby Kemper Collection
Gift of the R. C. Kemper Charitable Trust, 2008.18

Archie Scott **Gobber**

In Loving Memory of You, 2008
enamel on wood panels
80 x 144 inches
Museum purchase made possible
by gifts from the Collectors Forum and
the Sosland Acquisition Fund, 2008.26

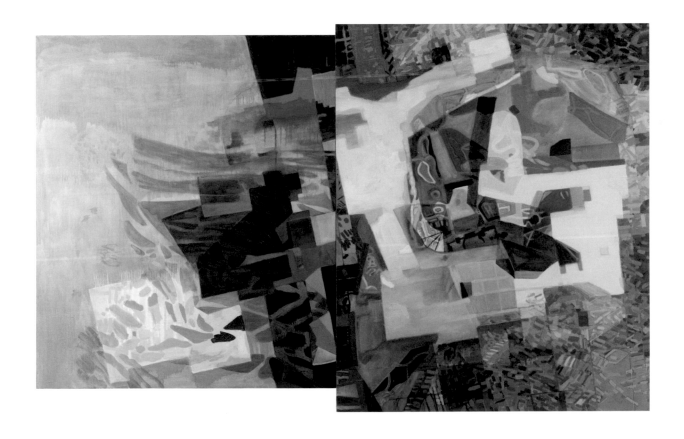

Barbara **Grad**

Plan B, 2010
oil on linen, diptych
68 x 94 inches
Gift of the artist in memory of
Ruth and Rubin Horwitz, 2011.12a–b

Nancy **Graves**

Immovable Iconography, 1990
paint and polychrome patina on aluminum, bronze, brass
24 x 22 x 12 inches
Bebe and Crosby Kemper Collection
Gift of the William T. Kemper Charitable Trust, UMB Bank, n.a.,
Trustee, 1995.34

Columniary, 1981
bronze
113 x 23 x 23 inches
Bebe and Crosby Kemper Collection
Museum purchase, Enid and Crosby Kemper
and William T. Kemper Acquisition Fund, 2004.24a–b

Red **Grooms**

Elvis, 1987
color lithograph, edition 66/75
44⅛ x 30⅛ inches
Bebe and Crosby Kemper Collection
Museum purchase made possible by a gift
from Bebe and Crosby Kemper in honor of
Cynthia Kemper Dietrich, 2011.13

Nabis, 1998
oil on wood
44¼ x 88¼ inches
Bebe and Crosby Kemper Collection
Gift of the Enid and Crosby Kemper Foundation, 1998.7

Ocean Waters / Monhegan Island   9/25/91   Alan Gussow

Alan **Gussow**

Ocean Waters / Monhegan Island, 1991
pastel on paper
38 x 50 inches
Bebe and Crosby Kemper Collection
Museum purchase made possible by a gift from
the R. C. Kemper Charitable Trust, 2010.1

Trenton Doyle **Hancock**

Good Vegan Progression #1, 2005
mixed media on felt
118 x 123 inches
Museum purchase, Enid and Crosby Kemper
and William T. Kemper Acquisition Fund
and Sosland Acquisition Fund, 2005.40

Duane **Hanson**

Salesman, 1992
paint, polyvinyl, clothing
68 x 17 x 14 inches
Bebe and Crosby Kemper Collection
Gift of the William T. Kemper Charitable Trust,
UMB Bank, n.a., Trustee, 1995.36

Grace **Hartigan**

The Massacre, 1952
oil on canvas
80 x 127¾ inches
Bebe and Crosby Kemper Collection
Gift of the Enid and Crosby Kemper Foundation, 1995.38

Marsden **Hartley**

Backwaters Up Millinocket Way, 1939—40
oil on millboard
22 x 28 inches
Bebe and Crosby Kemper Collection
Gift of the William T. Kemper Charitable Trust, UMB Bank, n.a.,
Trustee, 2003.2

Childe **Hassam**

Nude, Appledore, Isle of Shoals, 1913
oil on canvas
35⅝ x 25⅛ inches
Bebe and Crosby Kemper Collection
Gift of Mr. and Mrs. R. Crosby Kemper Jr., 2000.5

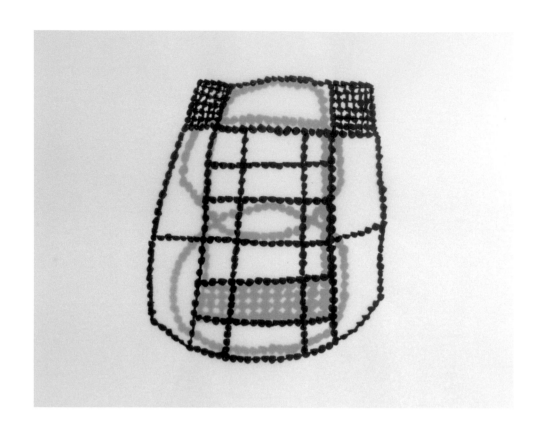

Susan **Hefuna**

Building, 2008
ink on tracing paper
21 x 27 inches
Bebe and Crosby Kemper Collection
Museum purchase made possible by a gift from
the R. C. Kemper Charitable Trust, 2011.14

Building, 2008
ink on tracing paper
21 x 27 inches
Bebe and Crosby Kemper Collection
Museum purchase made possible by a gift from
the R. C. Kemper Charitable Trust, 2011.15

Gottfried **Helnwein**

The Murmur of the Innocents 18, 2010
oil and acrylic on canvas
70 x 99¼ inches
Bebe and Crosby Kemper Collection
Museum purchase made possible by a gift
from the Enid and Crosby Kemper Foundation,
2011.16

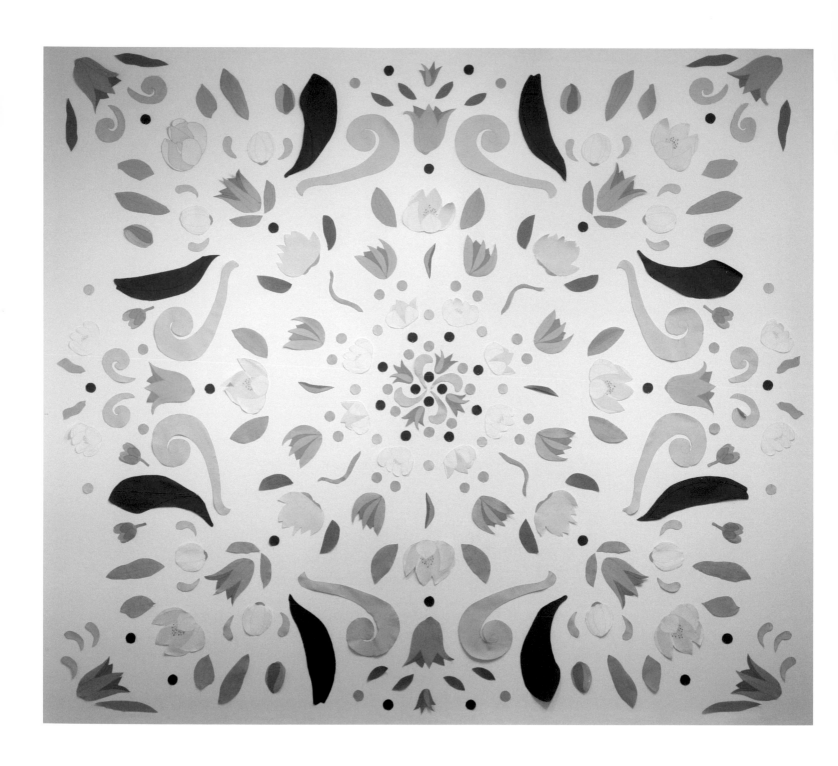

Ana Maria **Hernando**

Niña Sonando (Young Girl Dreaming), 2010
embroidered linen and stainless steel pins
132 x 148⅜ inches
Bebe and Crosby Kemper Collection
Museum purchase made possible by a gift from
the Enid and Crosby Kemper Foundation, 2011.18

Todd **Hido**

Untitled #3277, 2003
chromogenic color print mounted on aluminum,
edition 2/3 AP
20 x 24 inches
Museum purchase made possible by a gift from
Dr. Michael Bastasch, Dallas, Texas, 2005.22

Untitled #1975-a, 1996
chromogenic color print mounted on aluminum, edition 1/1 AP
38 x 30 inches
Museum purchase, Barbara Uhlmann Memorial Fund, 2005.21

Damien **Hirst**

Beautiful Divided Madness Slowly Creeping Painting, 2005
household gloss on canvas
36 x 52 inches
Bebe and Crosby Kemper Collection
Gift of the William T. Kemper Charitable Trust,
UMB Bank, n.a., Trustee, 2006.8

The Last Supper (details), 1999
13 screen prints, PP, edition of 150
60 x 40 inches each
Bebe and Crosby Kemper Collection
Museum purchase, Enid and Crosby Kemper and
William T. Kemper Acquisition Fund, 2003.18.1–13

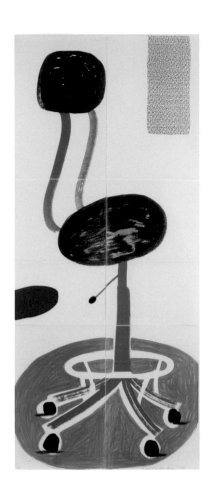

David **Hockney**

Office Chair, July 1988, 1988
color lithograph, edition 31/40
51 x 22 inches
Bebe and Crosby Kemper Collection
Gift of the William T. Kemper Charitable Trust,
UMB Bank, n.a., Trustee, 1995.41

Mountain from Stunt Road, 1990
oil on canvas
36 x 48 inches
Bebe and Crosby Kemper Collection
Gift of the William T. Kemper Charitable Trust,
UMB Bank, n.a., Trustee, 2005.13

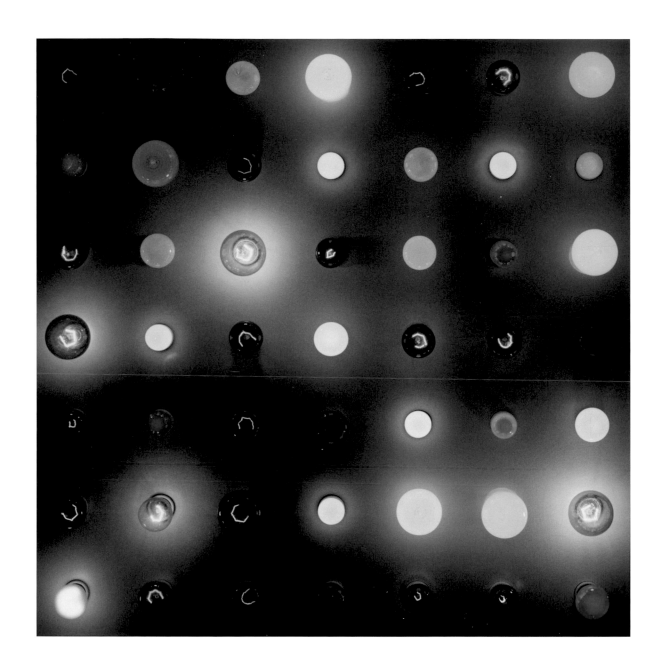

Jim **Hodges**

Dot, 1999
light bulbs and ceramic sockets on wood and metal panel
31½ x 31½ x 5 inches
Bebe and Crosby Kemper Collection
Gift of the William T. Kemper Charitable Trust, UMB Bank, n.a.,
Trustee, 1999.12

Hans **Hofmann**

Rising Sun, 1958
oil on canvas
60 x 72 inches
Bebe and Crosby Kemper Collection
Gift of the Enid and Crosby Kemper Foundation, 2002.12

Liu **Hong**

Beautiful Language No. 12, 2008
oil on canvas
70¾ x 50 inches
Bebe and Crosby Kemper Collection
Museum purchase made possible by a gift from
the R. C. Kemper Charitable Trust, 2009.18

Elizabeth **Huey**

The Visions of Charles Bonnet, 2007
acrylic and oil on wood panel
48 x 96 inches
Bebe and Crosby Kemper Collection
Gift of the R. C. Kemper Charitable Trust, 2008.16

Keith **Jacobshagen**

Quonset Hut N.E. of Ashland—72°—Listening to Miles 11.8.09, 2009
oil on paper
8 x 10 inches
Bebe and Crosby Kemper Collection
Museum purchase made possible by a gift from
the R. C. Kemper Charitable Trust, 2010.9

Near Holland—Scouting Panama, Hickman—73°—4:30–7:00 p.m., Grackles and Starlings Flocking, Oct 3, 2009, 2009
oil on paper
8 x 10 inches
Bebe and Crosby Kemper Collection
Museum purchase made possible by a gift from
the R. C. Kemper Charitable Trust, 2010.8

Luis **Jimenez**

Mesteño (Mustang), 1997–2001
fiberglass, acrylic urethane, light bulbs, AP 5
98 x 46 x 35 inches
Museum purchase made possible by a gift from
DST Systems, Inc., 2003.9

Jasper **Johns**

Spring, 1987
from the series *The Seasons*
etching and aquatint, edition 38/73
19½ x 13 inches
Bebe and Crosby Kemper Collection
Gift of the Enid and Crosby Kemper Foundation, 1995.46.1

Summer, 1987
from the series *The Seasons*
etching and aquatint, edition 38/73
19¾ x 13 inches
Bebe and Crosby Kemper Collection
Gift of the Enid and Crosby Kemper Foundation, 1995.46.2

Fall, 1987
from the series *The Seasons*
etching and aquatint, edition 38/73
19¼ x 13 inches
Bebe and Crosby Kemper Collection
Gift of the Enid and Crosby Kemper Foundation, 1995.46.3

Winter, 1987
from the series *The Seasons*
etching and aquatint, edition 38/73
19¼ x 13 inches
Bebe and Crosby Kemper Collection
Gift of the Enid and Crosby Kemper Foundation, 1995.46.4

Bo **Joseph**

Return to Plato's Cave, 2009
ink, watercolor, acrylic, oil pastel, tempera, pencil on joined paper
36½ x 76½ inches
Bebe and Crosby Kemper Collection
Museum purchase made possible by a gift from
the William T. Kemper Charitable Trust, UMB Bank, n.a., Trustee, 2012.4

Roberto **Juarez**

Granny Apples, 1995
from the series *They Entered the Road*
acrylic, charcoal, peat moss, rice paper on canvas
112 x 225 inches
Bebe and Crosby Kemper Collection
Gift of the William T. Kemper Charitable Trust,
UMB Bank, n.a., Trustee, 1997.13.1

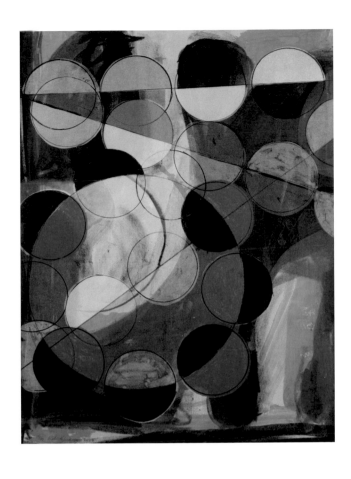

Heliopolis, 2008
color lithograph, edition 12/30
32 x 24 inches
Bebe and Crosby Kemper Collection
Museum purchase made possible by a gift from
the R. C. Kemper Charitable Trust, 2011.19

Flowers and Pearls VI, 2013
color monoprint on soft white Somerset book paper, edition 6/9
26¼ x 40 inches
Gift of Roberto Juarez and Shark's Ink. in honor of the
20th Anniversary of the Kemper Museum, 2013.7

Wolf **Kahn**

Out of the Bay, 1992
oil on canvas
14 x 22 inches
Bebe and Crosby Kemper Collection
Museum purchase made possible by a gift from
the Enid and Crosby Kemper Foundation, 1995.47

Alex **Katz**

Coleman Pond II, 1995
oil on canvas
96 x 72 inches
Bebe and Crosby Kemper Collection
Gift of the Enid and Crosby Kemper Foundation, 1997.3

Rockwell **Kent**

Adirondack Valley, Winter Night, 1945
oil on canvas
38 x 44 inches
Bebe and Crosby Kemper Collection
Museum purchase, Enid and Crosby Kemper and William T. Kemper Acquisition
Fund, with additional funds from the Enid and Crosby Kemper Foundation and
the William T. Kemper Charitable Trust, UMB Bank, n.a., Trustee, 2005.42

Martin **Kline**

Daydream for Pollock, 2009
encaustic on panel
32 x 32 inches
Bebe and Crosby Kemper Collection
Museum purchase made possible by a gift from the William T. Kemper
Charitable Trust, UMB Bank, n.a., Trustee, 2011.20

Susanne **Kühn**

Regina arbeitet (Regina Working), 2009
oil on canvas
78¾ x 90¾ inches
Museum purchase made possible by a gift from the
E. Kemper Carter and Anna Curry Carter Community
Memorial Trust, UMB Bank, n.a., Trustee, 2010.21

Anne geht Baden (Anne Goes Swimming), 2005
oil on canvas
86½ x 62¾ inches
Gift of Dean Valentine and Amy Adelson, 2009.19

Gaston **Lachaise**

Woman's Head, Long Neck, 1923
bronze, edition 4/12
11 x 7¾ x 9 inches
Gift of Beatrice Davis, Kansas City, Missouri, 2005.7

Magnolia **Laurie**

November Charlie (I am in distress and require immediate assistance), 2008
oil on panel
16 x 16 inches
Bebe and Crosby Kemper Collection
Museum purchase made possible by a gift from
the R. C. Kemper Charitable Trust, 2010.12

to abandon my vessel (ALFA CHARLIE), 2009
oil on panel
16 x 16 inches
Bebe and Crosby Kemper Collection
Museum purchase made possible by a gift from
the R. C. Kemper Charitable Trust, 2010.13

Nikki S. **Lee**

The Hispanic Project (20), 1998
chromogenic color print, edition 3/3
40 x 30 inches
Bebe and Crosby Kemper Collection
Museum purchase, Enid and Crosby Kemper and
William T. Kemper Acquisition Fund, 2006.14

Anthony **Lepore**

Untitled (Brooklyn, NY), 2005
pigment print, edition 1/10
27 x 34 inches
Gift of the artist and Marvelli Gallery, New York, 2009.1

Coney Island Aquarium, 2007
pigment print, edition 8/10
27 x 34 inches
Gift of the artist and Marvelli Gallery, New York, 2009.2

Linda **Lighton**

Mapped Flower, 1995
white earthenware, glaze, china paint
11¼ x 31 x 22 inches
Bebe and Crosby Kemper Collection
Museum purchase made possible by a gift from
the Enid and Crosby Kemper Foundation, 2007.16

Jacques **Lipchitz**

Bellerophon Taming Pegasus: Large Version, 1964–66
bronze, edition 1/2
179½ x 134 x 59 inches
Bebe and Crosby Kemper Collection
Gift of the William T. Kemper Charitable Trust, UMB Bank, n.a.,
Trustee, 2000.14

Hung **Liu**

Passage, 1999
oil on canvas
80 x 110 inches
Bebe and Crosby Kemper Collection
Museum purchase made possible by a gift from
the R. C. Kemper Jr. Charitable Trust, 2004.6

Untitled, 2004
from the series *Seven Poses*
pigment print with paper collage, edition 3/30
14 x 14 inches
Museum purchase made possible by a gift from
Jo and Bob Loyd, 2005.4.5

Untitled, 2004
from the series *Seven Poses*
pigment print with paper collage, edition 3/30
14 x 14 inches
Museum purchase made possible by a gift from
Jo and Bob Loyd, 2005.4.6

Hew **Locke**

Saturn, 2007
chromogenic color print, edition 2/3
90⅞ x 71¼ inches
Bebe and Crosby Kemper Collection
Museum purchase made possible by a gift from
the R. C. Kemper Charitable Trust, 2008.27

Tyger, Tyger, 2007
chromogenic color print, edition 1/3
90⅛ x 71¼ inches
Bebe and Crosby Kemper Collection
Museum purchase made possible by a gift from
the R. C. Kemper Charitable Trust, 2008.28

Morris **Louis**

Beth Rash, 1958–59
acrylic resin on canvas
98½ x 141¾ inches
Bebe and Crosby Kemper Collection
Museum purchase made possible by gifts from
Bebe and Crosby Kemper, the William T. Kemper
Charitable Trust, UMB Bank, n.a., Trustee, and by
additional funds from the Enid and Crosby Kemper
and William T. Kemper Acquisition Fund, 2002.30

Loretta **Lux**

Three Wishes, 2001
chromogenic color print, MP
19¼ x 19¼ inches
Bebe and Crosby Kemper Collection
Museum purchase made possible by a gift from
the Enid and Crosby Kemper Foundation, 2008.1

Neeta **Madahar**

Sustenance 79, 2003
from the series *Sustenance*
Iris print on Somerset Velvet paper, edition 8/15
35 x 47 inches
Bebe and Crosby Kemper Collection
Museum purchase, Enid and Crosby Kemper
and William T. Kemper Acquisition Fund, 2006.13

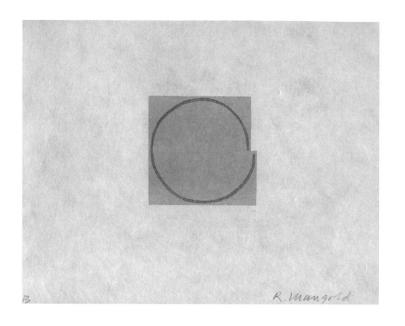

Robert **Mangold**

untitled (B), 2000
from the portfolio *Robert Mangold Prints, 1968–1998*,
published by Parasol Press, LTD
woodcut, edition 37/250
7¹⁵⁄₁₆ x 9¹⁵⁄₁₆ inches
Gift of Senator Thomas F. Eagleton, 2002.26.2

untitled (F), 2000
from the portfolio *Robert Mangold Prints, 1968–1998*,
published by Parasol Press, LTD
woodcut, edition 37/250
7¹⁵⁄₁₆ x 9¹⁵⁄₁₆ inches
Gift of Senator Thomas F. Eagleton, 2002.26.6

untitled (E), 2000
from the portfolio *Robert Mangold Prints, 1968–1998*,
published by Parasol Press, LTD
woodcut, edition 37/250
7¹⁵⁄₁₆ x 9¹⁵⁄₁₆ inches
Gift of Senator Thomas F. Eagleton, 2002.26.5

untitled (G), 2000
from the portfolio *Robert Mangold Prints, 1968–1998*,
published by Parasol Press, LTD
woodcut, edition 37/250
7¹⁵⁄₁₆ x 9¹⁵⁄₁₆ inches
Gift of Senator Thomas F. Eagleton, 2002.26.7

Joan **Mitchell**

Untitled, 1959—60
oil on canvas
76 x 114⅜ inches
Bebe and Crosby Kemper Collection
Gift of the Enid and Crosby Kemper Foundation, 1996.60

Lisette **Model**

Famous Gambler, Promenade des Anglais, Riviera, 1937
gelatin silver print
19½ x 15½ inches
Gift of Drs. Antonio and Luz Racela, 1997.29.9

Newspaper Man, Paris, ca. 1938
gelatin silver print
19½ x 15¾ inches
Gift of Drs. Antonio and Luz Racela, 1997.29.10

Abelardo **Morell**

Two Tall Books, 2002
gelatin silver print, edition 2/15
31¾ x 40 inches
Bequest of the Honorable Thomas F. Eagleton
and Barbara S. Eagleton, 2007.10

Malcolm **Morley**

Approaching Valhalla, 1998
oil on linen
102 x 79 inches
Collection of the Enid and Crosby Kemper Foundation, L2008.1

Richard **Mosse**

Men of Good Fortune, 2011
from the series *Infra*
digital color print, edition 1/2
71 x 89 inches
Bebe and Crosby Kemper Collection
Museum purchase made possible by a gift from
the Enid and Crosby Kemper Foundation, 2011.23

Alice **Neel**

Portrait of Sid Duffy, 1973
oil on canvas
46 x 32 inches
Bebe and Crosby Kemper Collection
Gift of the Enid and Crosby Kemper Foundation, 1995.56

Manuel **Neri**

Untitled, 1991
Carrara marble
91 x 27 x 23½ inches
Bebe and Crosby Kemper Collection
Gift of the Enid and Crosby Kemper Foundation, 1997.18

Louise **Nevelson**

Untitled, date unknown
painted wood
80 x 48 inches
Bebe and Crosby Kemper Collection
Gift of the Enid and Crosby Kemper Foundation, 2009.30

Dale **Nichols**

Earth to Rest, 1936
oil on canvas
30¼ x 40¼ inches
Bebe and Crosby Kemper Collection
Gift of the William T. Kemper Charitable Trust,
UMB Bank, n.a., Trustee, 2009.22

Wilbur **Niewald**

Still Life with Bowl of Apples and Grey Pitcher, 1999
oil on canvas
26 x 32 inches
Gift of Gerry and Wilbur Niewald in honor of the 20th
Anniversary of the Kemper Museum of Contemporary Art,
2013.12

Current River II, 1965
oil on canvas
54½ x 70½ inches
Gift of J. Scott Francis, Kansas City, Missouri,
in memory of Sally Kemper Wood, 2011.24

Kenneth **Noland**

Untitled (Rainbow), 1981
handmade paper
25 x 30 inches
Bebe and Crosby Kemper Collection
Gift of the William T. Kemper Charitable Trust,
UMB Bank, n.a., Trustee, 1995.57

Mysteries: Red Light, 1999
acrylic on canvas
60 x 60 inches
Bebe and Crosby Kemper Collection
Gift of the William T. Kemper Charitable Trust,
UMB Bank, n.a., Trustee, 2014.1

Maple and Cedar, Lake George, 1922
oil on canvas
25 x 20 inches
Gift of Mr. and Mrs. Gerald P. Peters, 2000.17

Yellow Jonquils #3, 1936
oil on canvas
30¼ x 40¼ inches
Bebe and Crosby Kemper Collection
Gift of the Enid and Crosby Kemper Foundation
and the R. C. Kemper Charitable Trust, 2005.12

Autumn Trees—The Chestnut Tree—Red, 1924
oil on canvas
36⅛ x 30 inches
Bebe and Crosby Kemper Collection
Partial and promised gift of the William T. Kemper
Charitable Trust, UMB Bank, n.a., Trustee, 2006.22

Claes **Oldenburg** and Coosje **van Bruggen**

Architect's Handkerchief, 1999
polyester gel coat and polyurethane clearcoat
on steel and fiber-reinforced polymers,
edition 3/3, 1 AP
149 x 144½ x 89 inches
Bebe and Crosby Kemper Collection
Museum purchase, Enid and Crosby Kemper
and William T. Kemper Acquisition Fund, with
additional funds provided by the Enid and
Crosby Kemper Foundation, 2006.17a–b

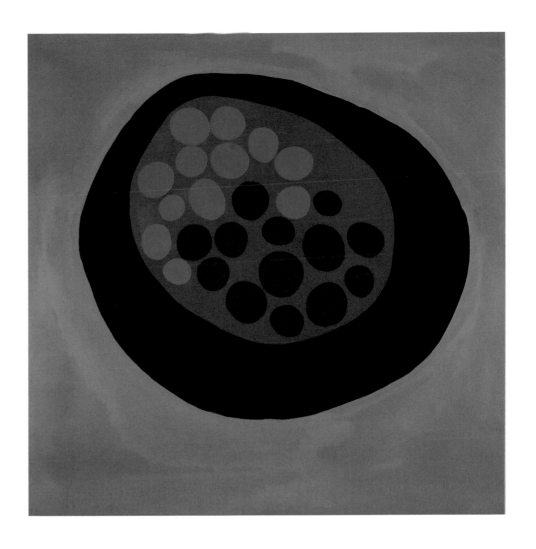

Jules **Olitski**

Prince Patutszky Pleasures, 1962
acrylic on canvas
89¾ x 88 inches
Bebe and Crosby Kemper Collection
Gift of the R. C. Kemper Charitable Trust, 2009.21

Eos the Titan, 2006
acrylic on steel
82 x 50 x 83 inches
Bebe and Crosby Kemper Collection
Museum purchase made possible by a gift from
the R. C. Kemper Charitable Trust, 2007.7

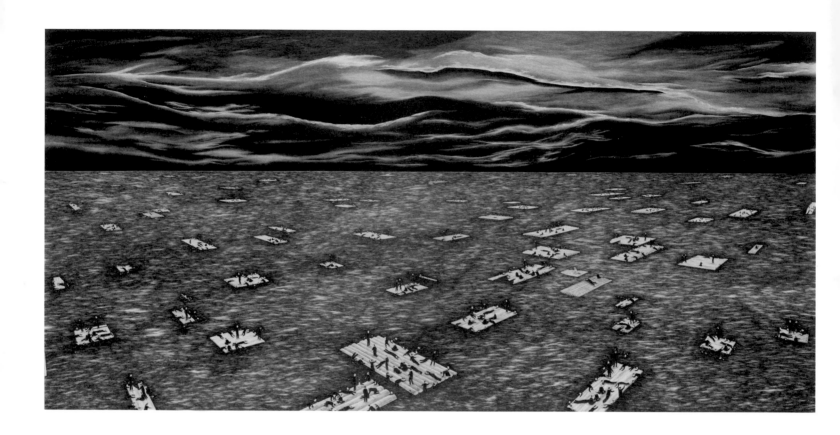

Robyn **O'Neil**

Masses and masses rove a darkened pool;
never is there laughter on this ship of fools, 2007
graphite on paper
79¾ x 161⅛ inches
Museum purchase made possible by a gift from the
Kearney Wornall Foundation, UMB Bank, n.a., Trustee,
2007.3

Tom **Otterness**

Crying Giant, 2002
bronze, edition 2/3
132 x 78 x 173 inches
Museum purchase made possible by a gift from the
Kearney Wornall Foundation, UMB Bank, n.a., Trustee,
and the Enid and Crosby Kemper Foundation, 2002.24a–b

Philip **Pearlstein**

Two Models on Kilim Rug with Mirror, 1983
acrylic on canvas
90 x 72 inches
Bebe and Crosby Kemper Collection
Gift of the Enid and Crosby Kemper Foundation, 1995.59

Jackson **Pollock**

untitled [Silver and Black Diptych], ca. 1950
oil on canvas, diptych
11½ x 17 inches
Promised gift of the Enid and Crosby Kemper Foundation,
L1999.1

Fairfield **Porter**

Wheat, 1960
oil on canvas
36 x 36 inches
Bebe and Crosby Kemper Collection
Gift of the Enid and Crosby Kemper Foundation, 1995.62

Robert **Rauschenberg**

Untitled, 1979
collodion transfer and fabric collage on paper
31 x 22 inches
Bebe and Crosby Kemper Collection
Gift of the William T. Kemper Charitable Trust,
UMB Bank, n.a., Trustee, 1995.64

Seminole Host, 1990
from the series *ROCI USA (Wax Fire Works)*
acrylic and wax on stainless steel, PP, edition of 22
72¾ x 96¾ inches
Bebe and Crosby Kemper Collection
Gift of the R. C. Kemper Charitable Trust, 2008.13

Michael **Rees**

Putto 2x2x4, 2005
animation and LuminOre on fiberglass
over expanded polystyrene foam and steel
192 x 122 x 175 inches, 1:48 min. loop
Museum purchase made possible by a gift from DST Systems, Inc.,
2005.1a—b

Paula **Rego**

Recreation, 1996
pastel on paper on aluminum
66⅝ x 51¼ inches
Bebe and Crosby Kemper Collection
Gift of the Enid and Crosby Kemper Foundation, 1997.4

Matt **Rich**

Double Twist, 2012
latex, acrylic, spray paint on cut paper and linen tape
43⅛ x 73¾ inches
Bebe and Crosby Kemper Collection
Museum purchase made possible by a gift from
the R. C. Kemper Charitable Trust, 2012.6

Matthew **Ritchie**

Experienced Time, 2003
enamel on Sintra and vinyl
102 x 384½ inches
Bebe and Crosby Kemper Collection
Museum purchase, Enid and Crosby Kemper and
William T. Kemper Acquisition Fund, 2004.9

Larry **Rivers**

Utamaro's Women, 1972–99
oil on canvas mounted on sculpted foam core
24 x 19 inches
Bebe and Crosby Kemper Collection
Museum purchase made possible by a gift from
the R. C. Kemper Charitable Trust, 2010.14

Norberto **Rodriguez**

OPEN 24 HRS, 2004
from the series *the gifts I could never give you*
neon lamps and Plexiglas, AP
18½ x 70½ x 3 inches
Bebe and Crosby Kemper Collection
Gift of Mr. and Mrs. R. Crosby Kemper Jr., 2005.37

Edward **Ruscha**

Purely Polyester, 1977
pastel on paper
23 x 29 inches
Museum purchase made possible in part by a gift
from the E. Kemper Carter and Anna Curry Carter
Community Memorial Trust, UMB Bank, n.a., Trustee,
2002.17

Lezley **Saar**

Geneva Saar Agustsson—Labeled Autistic, 1998
mixed media on canvas
80 x 48 x 4 inches
Bebe and Crosby Kemper Collection
Museum purchase made possible by a gift from the
William T. Kemper Charitable Trust, UMB Bank, n.a., Trustee, 2000.1

Lisa **Sanditz**

SubTropolis, 2006
acrylic on canvas
57 x 77 inches
Bebe and Crosby Kemper Collection
Museum purchase made possible by a gift from
the R. C. Kemper Jr. Charitable Trust, 2006.18

Michael **Schultz**

Belgium 2005, 2010
chromogenic print, edition 1/10
44 x 60 inches
Museum purchase made possible by a gift from the
Barbara Uhlmann Memorial Fund, on the occasion
of Paul Ulhmann Jr.'s 90th birthday, 2010.17

Cindy **Sherman**

Untitled Film Still #60, 1980
gelatin silver print, edition 2/3
40 x 30 inches
Bebe and Crosby Kemper Collection
Gift of the Enid and Crosby Kemper Foundation, 2014.2

Roger **Shimomura**

Untitled, 1984
acrylic on canvas
60½ x 72¼ inches
Bebe and Crosby Kemper Collection
Museum purchase, Enid and Crosby Kemper and
William T. Kemper Acquisition Fund, 2000.13

Mike **Sinclair**

Anne's Wedding, 2000
chromogenic color print, edition 2/25
20 x 24 inches
Bebe and Crosby Kemper Collection
Museum purchase, Enid and Crosby Kemper and
William T. Kemper Acquisition Fund, 2006.11

Las Vegas, Nevada, November, 2000
chromogenic color print, edition 1/10
24 x 38¼ inches
Bebe and Crosby Kemper Collection
Museum purchase, Enid and Crosby Kemper and
William T. Kemper Acquisition Fund, 2006.12

Aaron **Siskind**

untitled, ca. 1935
from the series *A Harlem Document*
gelatin silver print
8 x 11 inches
Gift of Drs. Antonio and Luz Racela, 1997.29.14

Wishing Tree (*The Most Crowded Block*), 1939
from the series *A Harlem Document*
gelatin silver print
6⅝ x 10⅛ inches
Gift of Drs. Antonio and Luz Racela, 1997.29.15

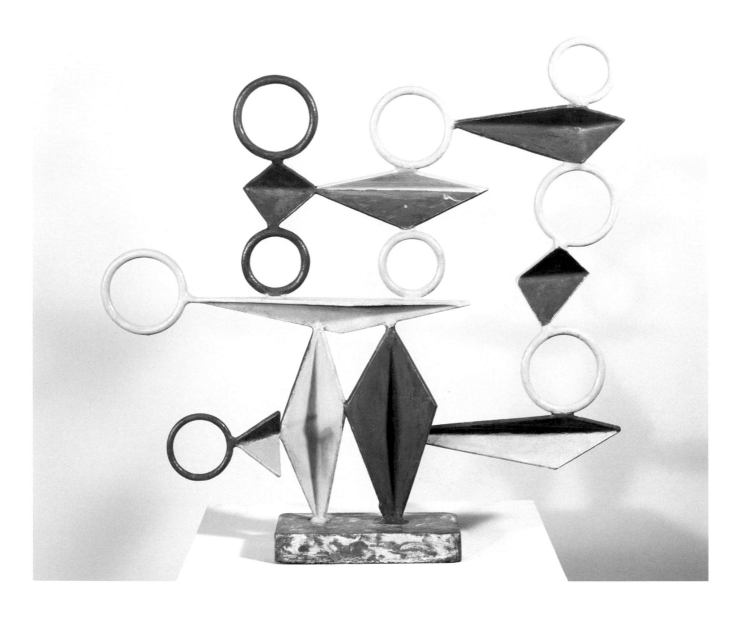

David **Smith**

Circles and Diamonds, 1951
oil on steel
30¾ x 32 x 6½ inches
Bebe and Crosby Kemper Collection
Gift of the Enid and Crosby Kemper Foundation, 1997.1.1

Untitled, 1951
watercolor on paper
18 x 23¾ inches
Bebe and Crosby Kemper Collection
Gift of the Enid and Crosby Kemper Foundation, 1997.1.2

Robert **Stackhouse**

Four Items, 1991
watercolor on paper
40 x 60 inches
Bebe and Crosby Kemper Collection
Gift of the William T. Kemper Charitable Trust,
UMB Bank, n.a., Trustee, 1995.69

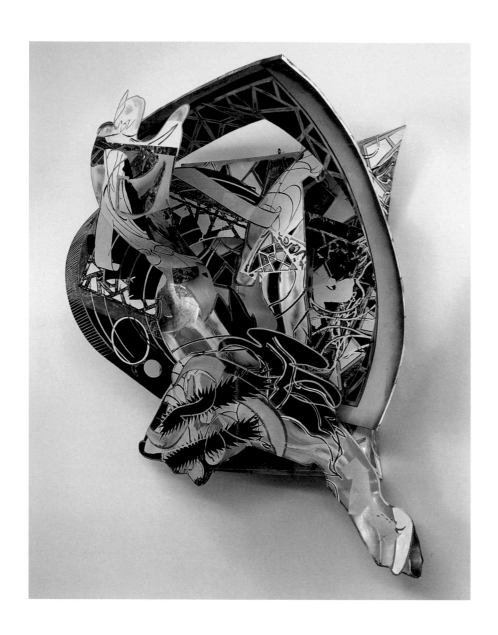

Frank **Stella**

The Prophet (D16, 2X), 1990
mixed media on aluminum
161½ x 109¾ x 68 inches
Gift of Mr. and Mrs. Ronald K. Greenberg,
the Enid and Crosby Kemper Foundation, and
the R. C. Kemper Charitable Trust, 1995.73a–f

Ohonoo, 1994
ink and paper collage
49 x 121½ inches
Bebe and Crosby Kemper Collection
Gift of the Enid and Crosby Kemper Foundation, 1998.9

Joseph **Stella**

Dance of Spring (Song of the Birds), 1924
oil on canvas
43⅜ x 32⅜ inches
Bebe and Crosby Kemper Collection
Gift of the Enid and Crosby Kemper Foundation, 2003.3

Alfred **Stieglitz**

Portrait of Georgia O'Keeffe, 1920
gelatin silver print
4½ x 3½ inches
Bebe and Crosby Kemper Collection
Gift of the Enid and Crosby Kemper Foundation,
2002.2

Equivalent, 1926 or 1929
gelatin silver print
4½ x 3⅝ inches
Bebe and Crosby Kemper Collection
Gift of the William T. Kemper Charitable Trust,
UMB Bank, n.a., Trustee, 2002.8

Marc **Swanson**

Descent of Civilization (Bison Memorial), 2010
bronze and limestone
120 x 107 x 36 inches
Museum purchase made possible by a gift from
DST Systems, Inc., 2010.18

Wayne **Thiebaud**

Cakes & Pies, 1994—95
oil on canvas
72 x 64 inches
Bebe and Crosby Kemper Collection
Gift of the Enid and Crosby Kemper Foundation, 1995.100

Day Streets, 1996
oil on canvas
59¾ x 48 inches
Bebe and Crosby Kemper Collection
Gift of the William T. Kemper Charitable Trust, UMB Bank, n.a.,
Trustee, and the R. C. Kemper Charitable Trust, 1996.69

River Divide, 2007
oil on canvas
60 x 48 inches
Bebe and Crosby Kemper Collection
Partial and promised gift of the Enid and Crosby Kemper Foundation,
2011.33

Yoshihiko **Ueda**

Quinalt No. 12, 1990–91
chromogenic color print, edition 1/8
50½ x 39½ inches
Museum purchase made possible by
a gift from Michael Klein, 2011.28

Ursula **von Rydingsvard**

Bowl with Sacks, 1998
cedar wood and graphite
35 x 60 x 60 inches
Bebe and Crosby Kemper Collection
Gift of the R. C. Kemper Charitable Trust, 1998.4a–c

Andy **Warhol**

Dennis Hopper, 1970
synthetic polymer paint and silkscreen ink on canvas
36 x 36 inches
Bebe and Crosby Kemper Collection
Museum purchase, Enid and Crosby Kemper and
William T. Kemper Acquisition Fund and a gift from
the R. C. Kemper Charitable Trust, 2002.16

Neil **Welliver**

Lower Ducktrap, 1978
oil on canvas
96 x 96 inches
Bebe and Crosby Kemper Collection
Gift of the R. C. Kemper Charitable Trust, 2009.31

Garry **Winogrand**

New York, 1968
from the portfolio *Women Are Beautiful*,
published 1981 by RFG, New York
gelatin silver print, edition 61/80
8¾ x 13 inches
Gift of Drs. Antonio and Luz Racela, 1998.14.5

Centennial Ball, Metropolitan Museum of Art, New York, 1969
from the portfolio *Women Are Beautiful*,
published 1981 by RFG, New York
gelatin silver print, edition 61/80
8¾ x 13⅛ inches
Gift of Drs. Pio and Esther Vilar, 1997.27.19

untitled, date unknown
from the portfolio *Women Are Beautiful*,
published 1981 by RFG, New York
gelatin silver print, edition 61/80
8¾ x 13⅛ inches
Gift of Drs. Antonio and Luz Racela, 1997.26.13

untitled, date unknown
from the portfolio *Women Are Beautiful*,
published 1981 by RFG, New York
gelatin silver print, edition 61/80
8¾ x 13 inches
Gift of Dr. and Mrs. John V. Knaus, 1997.28.17

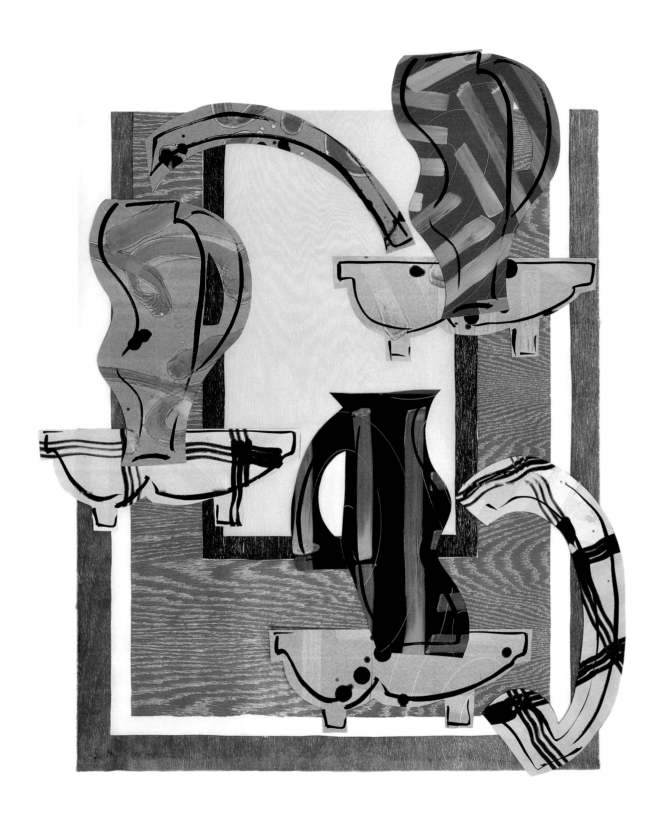

Betty **Woodman**

Vases and Windows IV-03, 2010
color woodcut and monoprint collage on paper
42¾ x 39½ inches
Bebe and Crosby Kemper Collection
Museum purchase made possible by a gift
from Bebe and Crosby Kemper in honor of
Sheila and Walter Dietrich, 2011.29

Andrew **Wyeth**

Fog Bell, 1967
watercolor on paper
27¼ x 18⅜ inches
Bebe and Crosby Kemper Collection
Gift of the William T. Kemper Charitable Trust,
UMB Bank, n.a., Trustee, 2012.22

Man and the Moon, 1990
egg tempera on Renaissance panel
30⅛ x 48 inches
Promised gift of the Enid and Crosby Kemper Foundation,
L2000.3

Jamie **Wyeth**

Stone Island, 1967
watercolor on paper
16¾ x 24⅜ inches
Bebe and Crosby Kemper Collection
Gift of Mr. and Mrs. R. Crosby Kemper Jr., 1995.82

Black Spruce, 1994
oil on panel
36 x 30 inches
Bebe and Crosby Kemper Collection
Gift of the William T. Kemper Charitable Trust,
UMB Bank, n.a., Trustee, 2002.3

Bones of a Whale, 2006
oil on canvas
60⅛ x 72⅛ inches
Bebe and Crosby Kemper Collection
Gift of the Enid and Crosby Kemper Foundation, 2006.19

Artists in the Collection

Magdalena Abakanowicz

Mark Adams

June Ahrens

Gary Akers

Josef Albers

Terry Allen

Jose Alvarez (D.O.P.A.)

Alvin Eli Amason

Gregory Amenoff

Barry Anderson

Peter Anton

Polly Apfelbaum

Ken Aptekar

Alexander Archipenko

Avigdor Arikha

L. C. Armstrong

Robert Arneson

Charles Arnoldi

Steven Assael

Ellen Auerbach

Milton Avery

Sally Michel Avery

Nicole Awai

Alice Baber

Francis Bacon

Bill Barminski

Tina Barney

Jennifer Bartlett

David Bates

Romare Bearden

Rosemarie Beck

José Bedia

Larry Bell

Philomene Bennett

Thomas Hart Benton

Robin Bernat

Harry Bertoia

Janice Biala

Elmer Bischoff

Ed Blackburn

Julie Blackmon

Rita Blitt

Diana Blok

Sonja Blomdahl

Claude Bogratchew

Christian Boltanski

Chakaia Booker

Fernando Botero

Louise Bourgeois

Claudio Bravo

Manuel Alvarez Bravo

David Brega

Doug Brega

James Brinsfield

James Brooks

Christopher Brown

Frederick James Brown

Richard Lotman Brown

Stephen Brown

Byron Browne

Jim Brustlein

John Buck

Dan Budnik

Charles Burchfield

Andy Burns

Deborah Butterfield

Paul Cadmus

Ingrid Calame

Alexander Calder

Harry Callahan

Jo Ann Callis

Morrie Camhi

Suzanne Caporael

Roberto Caracciolo

Annie Cardin

Squeak Carnwath

Brendan Cass

Marek Cecula

John Chamberlain

Robert Chambers

Dale Chihuly

William Christenberry

Dan Christensen

Christo and Jeanne-Claude

Carmen Louis Cicero

John Clem Clarke

William Clift

Chuck Close

Arthur Cohen

Jacob Collins

Stephen Conroy

Tom Corbin

Joseph Cornell

Petah Coyne

Ralston Crawford

James Croak

Russell Crotty

John Steuart Curry

Arthur B. Davies

Ian Davis

Lynn Davis

Stuart Davis

Elaine de Kooning

Willem de Kooning

Willem de Looper

Charles Demuth

Vincent Desiderio

Edwin Walter Dickinson

Philip-Lorca diCorcia

Richard Diebenkorn

Lesley Dill

Jim Dine

Mark di Suvero

Lois Dodd

Arthur Dove

Rackstraw Downes

Angela Dufresne

Friedel Dzubas

Michael Eastman

Robert Ebendorf

Dale Eldred

Marisol Escobar

Lalla Essaydi

Richard Estes

Terry Evans

Walker Evans

Robert Farber

Miller Farr

Nikolay Fechin

Keltie Ferris

John Fincher

Bean Finneran

Janet Fish

Caio Fonseca

Robert Forbes

Nate Fors

Chuck Forsman

Eric Forstmann

Angela Fraleigh

Linda Francis

Sam Francis

Mary Frank

Helen Frankenthaler

Antonio Frasconi

David Fredenthal

Douglass Freed

Jane Freilicher

Till Freiwald

Elsa Freund

Arnold Friedman

Gajin Fujita

Hope Gangloff

Gao Brothers

Paul Georges

Robert Gil de Montes

David James Gilhooly

William Glackens

Archie Scott Gobber

Joel Goldblatt

Nan Goldin

Robert Goodnough

Arshile Gorky

Barbara Grad

Robert Graham

Nancy Graves

Elliott Green

Jill Greenberg

Stephen Greene

Kojo Griffin

Thomasin Grim

Red Grooms

William Gropper

Alan Gussow

Trenton Doyle Hancock

Duane Hanson

Mary Harden

Grace Hartigan

Leon Hartl

Marsden Hartley

Burt Hasen

Childe Hassam

James Havard

Susan Hefuna

Bruce Helander

Al Held

John Heliker

Gottfried Helnwein

Ana Maria Hernando

Matthias Herrmann

Todd Hido

Fannie Hillsmith

Damien Hirst

David Hockney

Jim Hodges

Howard Hodgkin

Richard Hodgman

Hans Hofmann

Tom Holland

Liu Hong

Peregrine Honig

Charles Hopkinson

Elizabeth Huey

Jack Hughes

Bill Jacklin

Keith Jacobshagen

Frederic James

Marcus Jansen

Virginia Jaramillo
Luis Jimenez
Jasper Johns
Bo Joseph
Roberto Juarez
Wolf Kahn
John Kalymnios
Alex Katz
Ellsworth Kelly
Rockwell Kent
R. B. Kitaj
Martin Kline
Jutta Koether
Arthur Kraft
Barbara Kreft
Irving Kriesberg
Susanne Kühn
Walt Kuhn
Robert Kushner
Gaston Lachaise
David Lan-Bar
Betty Lane
Julio Larraz
Magnolia Laurie
Elizabeth Layton
Blanche Lazzell
Nikki S. Lee
John Lees
Anthony Lepore
David Levine
Joan Levy
Roy Lichtenstein
Linda Lighton
Anne Lindberg
Jacques Lipchitz
Beth Lipman
Hung Liu

Hew Locke
Morris Louis
Jean Lowe
Michael Lucero
Deborah Luster
Loretta Lux
Lee Lyon
Mike Lyon
Chris MacDonald
Stanton Macdonald-Wright
John Mackiewicz
Neeta Madahar
Marco Maggi
Robert Mangold
Larry Mantello
Robert Mapplethorpe
Lou Marak
Carlo Maria Mariani
John Marin
Richard Mayhew
Michael Mazur
Mara McAfee
Catherine McCarthy
Michael McClure
Christina McPhee
Julie Mehretu
Hugh Merrill
Joel Meyerowitz
Greg Miller
Dean Mitchell
Joan Mitchell
Lisette Model
John J. Moore
Abelardo Morell
Malcolm Morley
Richard Mosse
Robert Motherwell

Catherine Murphy
Json Myers
Bruce Nauman
Alice Neel
Joan Nelson
Manuel Neri
Louise Nevelson
Dale Nichols
Wilbur Niewald
Costantino Nivola
Kenneth Noland
Georgia O'Keeffe
Claes Oldenburg
   and Coosje van Bruggen
Jules Olitski
Nathan Oliveira
Robyn O'Neil
Julia Oschatz
Tom Otterness
Frank Owen
Anne Packard
Cynthia Packard
Tommy Dale Palmore
Sharon Patten
Philip Pearlstein
Judy Pfaff
Bernard Pfriem
Pablo Picasso
Jaume Plensa
Paul Pletka
Reginald Pollack
Jason Pollen
Jackson Pollock
Fairfield Porter
Zigmunds Priede
Nicholas Prior
Liz Whitney Quisgard

Peter Ralston

Robert Rauschenberg

Michael Rees

Paula Rego

Paul Resika

Matt Rich

Judy Rifka

Matthew Ritchie

Larry Rivers

Norberto Rodriguez

Milton Rogovin

Greg Rose

Rosebee

Aura Rosenberg

Terry Rosenberg

James Rosenquist

Alvin Ross

Edward Ruscha

Lezley Saar

Jim Sajovic

Tomás Sánchez

Lisa Sanditz

Melanie Schiff

Tobias Schneebaum

Michael Schultz

Sandra Scolnik

Sean Scully

Ben Shahn

Charles Sheeler

Bill Shepherd

Cindy Sherman

Roger Shimomura

Anne Siems

Burton Silverman

Hans Silvester

Mike Sinclair

Anna-Maria Sircello

Aaron Siskind

Hunt Slonem

Clive Smith

David Smith

Esther Solondz

Keith Sonnier

Robert Stackhouse

Julian Stanczak

Robert W. Stark III

Irma Starr

Saul Steinberg

Michael Steiner

Frank Stella

Joseph Stella

Joel Sternfeld

Alfred Stieglitz

Bruce Stillman

John Storrs

Paul Strand

Robert Sudlow

Do-Ho Suh

Donald Sultan

Marc Swanson

Tomoko Takahashi

Reuben Tam

Wayne Thiebaud

Arthur Tress

Cy Twombly

Yoshihiko Ueda

Manolo Valdés

Vandiver

Gregorio Vardanega

Christian Vincent

Andrea Vizzini

Ursula von Rydingsvard

Robert Walden

Joe Walters

Andy Warhol

Jaimie Warren

William Wegman

Kurt Weiser

Neil Welliver

Stephen Westfall

John Whalley

Hiram Williams

Christopher Wilmarth

Jane Wilson

Garry Winogrand

Paul Wonner

Betty Woodman

Andrew Wyeth

Henriette Wyeth

Jamie Wyeth

Bruce Yonemoto

Stephen Scott Young

Joe Zucker

Selected Exhibitions
1994–2014

1994–2003: Selected Exhibitions

organized by the Kemper Museum of Contemporary Art

1994

A Building of the Spirit

October 2, 1994–April 23, 1995
This exhibition documented the conception, planning, and construction of the Kemper Museum of Contemporary Art. Central to the presentation were architectural drawings by designer Gunnar Birkerts, representing the evolution of design phases of his firm's development of the project.

Museum model from *A Building of the Spirit* (1994–95)

1995

Patrick T. Dougherty: Colonnade

November 1995–May 1996
For his site-specific installation at the Kemper Museum, Patrick Dougherty created five enormous cocoon-like structures made from local elm and dogwood saplings. During a three-week residency, and using no glue, wire, or rope, he "wove" together the *Colonnade* and the Museum's entrance columns.

1996

Aziz + Cucher: Less Is Often More

April 13–June 16, 1996
The collaborative team of Anthony Aziz and Sammy Cucher used computers to erase the facial features (eyes, mouth, nostrils) of people's portraits. The results were unexpected and touched on the mystery of our continuing fascination with defining what makes us human, what is the source of "personality."

Guerrilla Girls: Posters of Protest

April 13–May 4, 1996
In conjunction with the Seventh Annual Culture Under Fire, a celebration of freedom of expression, the Kemper Museum installed a series of Guerrilla Girls posters that challenge the art world's representation of women and other marginalized cultures.

Reality Bites: Realism in Contemporary Art

May 4–June 23, 1996
This group exhibition featured paintings in a realistic style carrying a satirical "bite," altering our view of traditional realistic painting. Artists included Kerry James Marshall, Laurie Hogin, Ida Applebroog, and Catherine Murphy, among others.

Robert Rauschenberg: Major Printed Works, 1962–1995

June 8–August 11, 1996
Robert Rauschenberg was arguably one of the most influential and innovative printmakers in American art. This exhibition explored his contributions to printmaking through nearly four decades of his work.

Frank Stella
September 7–November 24, 1996
This exhibition featured Frank Stella's large mixed-media prints, including several from the *Moby Dick* series, in which he named the works after a character or episode in Herman Melville's classic novel.

Visualize the Art Guys
October 4–December 1, 1996
The Art Guys' performance and installation art danced on the edge of absurdity, including a penny column, a sliced-cheese grid, and making music by wrapping interior architectural features of the Museum in industrial plastic wrap.

An American Premiere: Chihuly Over Venice
December 15, 1996–March 16, 1997
Dale Chihuly created fourteen "Chandeliers" in glass factories in Finland, Ireland, Mexico, and Italy. They were originally installed over the canals in Venice.

Frank Stella (1996), installation view

1997

Roberto Juarez: They Entered the Road
August 10, 1997–February 1, 1998 (also December 10, 2004–February 27, 2005)
Juarez's immense paintings honored the memories of his sister, her daughter, and three close friends who died of AIDS. Nature's abundance—flowers, fruits, and natural materials—encouraged reflection on our passage through the physical world into another.

Out of Eden
September 6–November 30 , 1997
This group exhibition addressed our paradoxical relationship to nature, and specifically to the garden. Artists included Maura Bendett, Antonio Girbes, David Kroll, Eleanor Miller, Alison Moritsugu, Janet Pihlblad, Anne Siems, Maria Tomasula, Darren Waterston, and Andrew Young.

Dale Chihuly, *Palazzo Ducale* (1996), in *An American Premiere: Chihuly Over Venice* (1996–97)

1998

Christian Boltanski: So Far

February 21–May 3, 1998

Christian Boltanski's installation of shadow figures and *Monuments* used ephemeral materials such as newspaper clippings, snapshots, clothing, candles, and light bulbs to evoke a profound and disturbing archive of social, cultural, ethnic, and personal histories.

Christian Boltanski: So Far (1998), installation view

Sharon Lockhart

June 19–August 23, 1998

Sharon Lockhart's large-scale photographic portraits seemed to draw inspiration from seventeenth-century Dutch and eighteenth-century British portraiture and the atmospheric paintings of Caspar David Friedrich.

Liza Lou: Back Yard and Kitchen

July 25–October 18, 1998

Liza Lou's monumental projects *Back Yard* and *Kitchen* were quintessential tableaux of American life, completely rendered in glass beads. Conceived as companion pieces, the two created a luminously sparkling domestic setting.

Shahzia Sikander: Drawings and Miniatures

November 13, 1998–January 10, 1999

Pakistani American artist Shahzia Sikander adapted the techniques and images of Indian miniature painting in her own miniature and large-scale paintings. Sikander also produced a mural as an artist in residence at the Kemper Museum.

Michael Shaughnessy: Tir Dhúchais (homeland)

November 13, 1998–January 31, 1999

Michael Shaughnessy's installation was a collaboration between the artist and Museum visitors, who helped construct his abstract sculptures using ordinary hay. The resulting works took the form of two enormous wheels and several "hay lines."

Liza Lou, Kitchen (1991–96), in Liza Lou: Back Yard and Kitchen *(1998)*

Michael Shaughnessy, *Tir Dhúchais (homeland)* (1998)

1999

Kendall Buster: Sitelines and Suitors
July 30–October 24, 1999
Kendall Buster created new works for this exhibition during an artist residency at the Kemper Museum. Her sleek monumental sculptures suggested enormous seedpods, while her bulbous vessel forms emphasized notions of exterior and interior space.

Kathryn Spence: Wild
July 30–October 24, 1999
Kathryn Spence's tender yet haunting sculptures suggested that there is life and memory in the materials that become discards. Spence rendered pigeons out of newspapers, shaping them with tiny wires and bits of string, and covered pastel stuffed animals in old bathrobes and then built them up with mud.

Tina Barney: Familiar Records
August 27–November 14, 1999
Tina Barney's photographs of her wealthy New England family documented their daily lives and social rituals as well as the complex relationships played out between family members.

2000

The Lighter Side of Bay Area Figuration
April 7–June 18, 2000
This exhibition examined Bay Area figurative art from the late 1950s to 2000. Focusing on humorous and whimsical work, the exhibition featured 56 paintings, drawings, and sculptures by Robert Arneson, Elmer Bischoff, David Park, Wayne Thiebaud, and many others. The exhibition traveled to the San Jose Museum of Art, California.

Kendall Buster: Sitelines and Suitors (1999), installation view

Deborah Willis: Tied to Memory
May 5–July 16, 2000
Photographer and photo archivist Deborah Willis printed images, some taken by her and some appropriated from others, on photo-sensitive linen sewn into quilts. The images recovered and reshaped memories, becoming hybrid histories open to interpretation.

John Bisbee: Field
June 30–September 3, 2000
John Bisbee's formal sculpture, a massive site-specific installation made of ten-inch spikes and other metal objects, was both compellingly beautiful and seemingly dangerous.

Robert Therrien
June 30–September 3, 2000
Robert Therrien examined the interplay of proportion and our relationship to objects in his gigantic helix sculptures made of camp beds. His massively scaled object impacted our own relationship to our bodies and the world around us.

Sandra Scolnik, *Self-Portrait, Undeveloped* (2000), in *Sandra Scolnik: Self-Portraits* (2000–2001)

Sandra Scolnik: Self-Portraits
October 13, 2000–January 7, 2001
Sandra Scolnik's small, meticulously detailed oil paintings expressed her internal investigation of the self, memory, and experience.

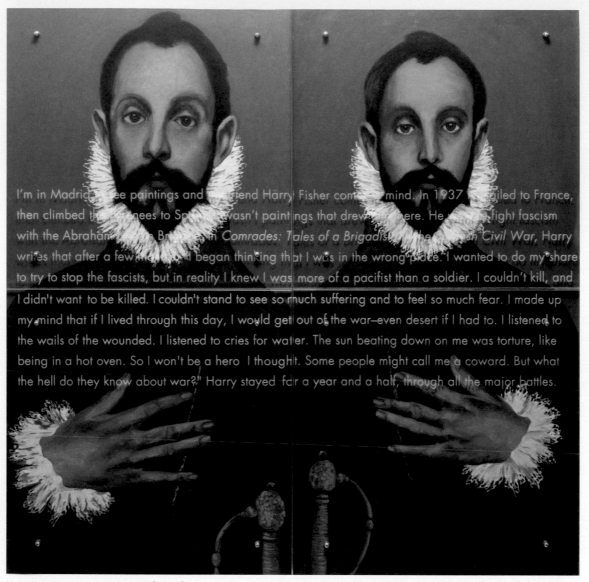

I'm in Madrid to see paintings and my friend Harry Fisher comes to mind. In 1937 he sailed to France, then climbed the Pyrenees to Spain. It wasn't paintings that drew him there. He came to fight fascism with the Abraham Lincoln Brigade. In *Comrades: Tales of a Brigadist in the Spanish Civil War*, Harry writes that after a few months, I began thinking that I was in the wrong place. I wanted to do my share to try to stop the fascists, but in reality I knew I was more of a pacifist than a soldier. I couldn't kill, and I didn't want to be killed. I couldn't stand to see so much suffering and to feel so much fear. I made up my mind that if I lived through this day, I would get out of the war—even desert if I had to. I listened to the wails of the wounded. I listened to cries for water. The sun beating down on me was torture, like being in a hot oven. So I won't be a hero I thought. Some people might call me a coward. But what the hell do they know about war?" Harry stayed for a year and a half, through all the major battles.

Ken Aptekar, *I'm in Madrid* (1999), in *Ken Aptekar: Painting Between the Lines, 1990–2000* (2001)

2001

Kojo Griffin
January 12–April 8, 2001
Kojo Griffin's layered, large-scale paintings revealed his fascination with the workings of the human psyche, his concern for his young children, and his memories of childhood.

Marco Maggi: Global Myopia
April 13–July 8, 2001
Marco Maggi worked with the most prosaic materials, such as aluminum foil and apples, to create intimate, labor-intensive works that seemed to speak a secret language. This was the first solo museum exhibition in the United States for Uruguayan-born Maggi.

Ken Aptekar: Painting Between the Lines, 1990–2000
September 16–December 2, 2001
This ten-year retrospective exhibition unraveled the often-autobiographical stories in Ken Aptekar's work, which had been incorporating text on glass since 1990. This exhibition traveled to the College of Wooster Art Museum, Ohio, and the Muscarelle Museum of Art, Virginia.

Michal Rovner: Works
October 12, 2001–January 6, 2002
Israeli-born Michal Rovner examined the borders of places, ideas, and media through video, film, and photography. Her beautiful yet ambiguous images imparted a tension of foreboding or violence.

Bruce Yonemoto: Screen Gems
December 14, 2001–March 10, 2002
Working with screens, monitors, imagery, objects, and ideas from video, film, television, and popular culture, Yonemoto examined recurring themes of memory, the construction of identity, and his third-generation Japanese-American heritage.

2002

Alex Katz: Small Paintings
March 22–June 2, 2002
Co-curated by the Addison Gallery of American Art, the Kemper Museum of Contemporary Art, and the Whitney Museum of American Art, this exhibition of approximately eighty works focused on the achievement and significance of Alex Katz's small paintings, the first American museum exhibition to do so.

Todd Hido: Open House
April 12–July 7, 2002
Todd Hido's color-saturated, nocturnal photographs of houses suggested the presence of absence and the physical and psychological effects of night.

Frederick J. Brown: Portraits in Jazz, Blues, and Other Icons
June 16–September 1, 2002
This exhibition drew together more than thirty paintings celebrating individuals who have shaped American cultural life and demonstrated Brown's impact as a prominent and prolific portrait painter. The exhibition traveled to the New Orleans Museum of Art, Louisiana, and the Studio Museum in Harlem, New York.

Bruce Yonemoto, *The Wedding* (1999), in *Bruce Yonemoto: Screen Gems* (2001–?)

Do-Ho Suh: The Perfect Home
December 20, 2002–March 2, 2003
Do-Ho Suh's sculptural installation explored the disparate notions of the individual and personal space in Eastern and Western cultures, and examined his experience of transcultural displacement as a Korean living in the United States.

Sharon Louden: The Attenders
March 14–May 25, 2003
Sharon Louden altered the gallery space using hundreds of thousands of strands of thin black and gray monofilament that looked like hair or some other natural fiber. Using an industrial material that viewers could touch, Louden questioned the preciousness of materials. This was her first solo museum exhibition.

Do-Ho Suh: The Perfect Home (2002–3), installation view

Russell Crotty, *Summer Triangle Over Chumash Wilderness* (2003),
in *Russell Crotty: Globe Drawings* (2003)

Russell Crotty: Globe Drawings

April 11–July 6, 2003
This exhibition included several new globe
drawings resulting from Russell Crotty's
studies of star clusters, constellations,
and planets as seen from the Solstice Peak
Observatory, which he built on 130 acres
in the Santa Monica Mountains.

Wayne Thiebaud: Fifty Years of Painting

June 6–August 31, 2003
This exhibition highlighted the work of
this profoundly influential and inventive
painter, demonstrating his contributions

to American popular culture and art
history. Many of the works in this
exhibition were from the Thiebaud
family's collection.

Jean Lowe: The Course of the Empire

September 14–November 30, 2003
Jean Lowe used papier-mâché, paint,
canvas, enamel, and resin to create an
installation of life-size, elaborately
decorated salon rooms, drawing on
eighteenth- and nineteenth-century
French design. Lowe's social and cultural
critiques were "hidden" in plain view.

2004–14: Selected Exhibitions

2004

Amy Cutler
April 9–July 11, 2004
Amy Cutler's finely crafted and highly detailed paintings and drawings brought to mind children's illustrations from Brothers Grimm fairytales. While not meant to be literal translations of children's stories, they spoke to the dark and quirky tradition of storytelling.

Polly Apfelbaum
June 4–September 5, 2004
This exhibition, organized by Philadelphia's Institute of Contemporary Art, featured Polly Apfelbaum's "fallen paintings," hybrid works of rare beauty that exist somewhere between painting, sculpture, and installation. Arranged on the floor in indeterminate shapes, Apfelbaum's forms comprised intricate, nearly psychedelic layers of dyed fabric.

Stained: The Art of Judith Schaechter
October 15, 2004–January 9, 2005
Judith Schaechter's works recalled the centuries-old medium of stained glass, enhanced by the glow of the modern-day electric light box. Schaechter's well-crafted parables suggested stories in which the protagonist overcomes an emotional or personal tragedy.

Out of Nature: Works by John Kalymnios
December 10, 2004–February 27, 2005
John Kalymnios's kinetic sculptures employed low-tech mechanics, video, and photography to toy with our perception and to become sensory experiences. His images, drawn primarily from nature, created a hypnotic sense of space.

2005

New Works by Mark Sheinkman
January 14–April 10, 2005
Sheinkman's works on canvas explored the possibilities of abstraction through classic elements of drawing. In his experimental line compositions, he blended sculptural and architectural features with his unique method of abstract painting.

Teresa Hubbard / Alexander Birchler: Editing the Dark
March 11–May 15, 2005
The high-definition video installations of Teresa Hubbard and Alexander Birchler commanded a strong sense of nontraditional storytelling. Influenced by Alfred Hitchcock films, their uncanny scenes depicted people in indeterminate yet familiar settings.

Teresa Hubbard and Alexander Birchler, still from *House with Pool* (2004), in *Teresa Hubbard / Alexander Birchler: Editing the Dark* (2005)

Naomi Fisher: Clear Cut
April 15–July 10, 2005
Naomi Fisher created psychologically and sexually charged drawings and photographs in which tropical landscape, decorative pattern, and fairytale figures collided in nightmarish scenarios of brilliantly hued images of women in menacing nature scenes.

Past in Reverse: Contemporary Art of East Asia (2005), installation view

Past in Reverse: Contemporary Art of East Asia

June 3–August 28, 2005
Organized by the San Diego Museum of Art, this exhibition presented works by more than twenty important and cutting-edge Chinese, Japanese, Taiwanese, and Korean artists and artist groups whose influence expressed their respective cultural and artistic heritages.

Strange Passages: An Installation by Maria Park

July 15–October 9, 2005
Maria Park used a combination of media and techniques—including acrylic on Acrylite, collage, and multicolored vinyl applied directly to the wall—to create environments of speed and digitized experience. Her fantastical landscapes unfolded like the sequence of a filmstrip to tell a story of time and place.

Petah Coyne: Above and Beneath the Skin

September 16–November 27, 2005
Organized by the Albright-Knox Art Gallery, this retrospective of work by Petah Coyne chronicled the artist's evolution from the late 1980s to 2005. The exhibition featured photographs and sculptures combining both figurative and abstract traditions.

Nikki S. Lee: Parts

October 14–December 11, 2005
Korean-born Nikki S. Lee examined the construction and interpretation of identity in conceptually based works that combined performance and photography. Lee documented her transformed appearance and assimilation into various subcultures and social and ethnic groups and focused on how identity is understood through the male/female relationship.

foldoverfold: Marcie Miller Gross
December 16, 2005–January 29, 2006
Marcie Miller Gross used nearly six thousand new cotton huck towels to create an environment that simultaneously explored spatial dynamics, the hidden histories of labor, and the poetic possibilities of utilitarian objects. This was her first solo museum exhibition.

Decelerate
December 16, 2005–February 19, 2006
Decelerate explored the cultural trend of "slowing down" to a more attuned state. From the very simple to the extremely complex, works by ten artists—Colby Caldwell, Augusto Di Stefano, Jacob El Hanani, Tony Feher, Anne Lindberg, Rei Naito, Sheila Pepe, Michelle Segre, Jennifer Steinkamp, and Yoshihiro Suda—were included in the exhibition.

Anne Lindberg, *democracy* (2005), in *Decelerate* (2005–6)

Marcie Miller Gross, *Intersection* (2005), in *foldoverfold: Marcie Miller Gross* (2005–6)

2006

Kurt Lightner: Five Acres
February 3–April 2, 2006
While grounded in the twenty-first century, Kurt Lightner's images recalled the varied history of American nature painting—from the awe-inspiring works of the Hudson River School artists to the watercolors of early American Modernist painter Charles Burchfield.

Ping-Pong Diplomacy: Stephen Hendee & Phoebe Washburn
March 11–May 14, 2006
Stephen Hendee and Phoebe Washburn took a historic 1971 table tennis tournament as their point of reference for two major installations with, at their juncture, a ping-pong arena replete with a fully functional game table and bleachers to be used by Museum visitors.

Ryan Humphrey: Empty Thoughts, Lame Excuses, and Decorative Lies
April 7–July 2, 2006
Coupling nostalgia for pop culture and irreverence for the history of art, sculptor and installation artist Ryan Humphrey's bold and energetic "customized" works derived from vintage car parts. This was Humphrey's first solo museum exhibition.

Capturing Nureyev: James Wyeth Paints the Dancer
June 2–August 20, 2006
Upon meeting the celebrated Russian dancer Rudolf Nureyev in 1974, James Wyeth was captivated by the beauty of dance as well as Nureyev's charismatic personality and exceptional talent. A friendship and fruitful collaboration resulted, inspiring Wyeth to produce more than thirty-five paintings and drawings of Nureyev.

Elissa Armstrong: Objects of Innocence and Experience
July 7–October 1, 2006
Elissa Armstrong's clay and plaster creatures from ceramic hobby molds were festooned with thick, garish glazes, glitter, decals, and felt, creating an aesthetic that subverts the history of decorative objects. This was her first solo museum exhibition.

Zephyr: Paintings by Gajin Fujita
September 8–November 5, 2006
Zephyr surveyed nearly a decade of Gajin Fujita's provocative and visually stunning paintings, elaborate fusions of contemporary urban street life and traditional Japanese iconography. This was Fujita's first major solo museum exhibition.

Lisa Sanditz, *Oklahoma City on New Year's Eve* (2005), in *Lisa Sanditz: Flyover* (2006–7)

Lisa Sanditz: Flyover
October 6, 2006–January 7, 2007
Painter Lisa Sanditz's exuberant and engaging landscapes mixed the homespun aesthetic of folk art with the calculated gestures of postmodernism. This was Sanditz's first solo museum exhibition.

Jennifer Steinkamp, *The Wreck of the Dumaru* (2004), installation view, in *Jennifer Steinkamp* (2007)

2007

Jennifer Steinkamp
February 16–May 13, 2007
One of the most important video and new media artists of her generation, Jennifer Steinkamp melded aspects of computer animation, digital media, experimental film, architecture, and design for the works in this exhibition. The exhibition was organized by the San Jose Museum of Art, California.

Phantasmania
June 1–August 19, 2007
Phantasmania featured paintings, drawings, sculptures, and installations by seventeen young, emerging artists responding to the pervasive climate of war, globalization, and the rise of mediated information and experience.

Backstage Pass: Collecting Art in Kansas City
September 7–November 4, 2007
This exhibition offered Museum visitors a rare opportunity to view works of art from private collections (normally housed in homes and offices) paired with examples by the same artists from the Kemper Museum's Permanent Collection. The diversity and quality of the works spoke to Kansas City's rich history of supporting the visual arts through public and private patronage.

Michael Vasquez: Authority Figures
October 5–December 30, 2007
Michael Vasquez's gestural multimedia paintings depicted the vibrant energy found in the artist's urban Florida neighborhood. His portraits of friends and acquaintances affiliated with Miami street gangs captured the social dynamics of gang culture while examining issues of identity, community, ritual, and stereotypes of urban youth.

Life After Death: New Leipzig Paintings from the Rubell Family Collection
November 16, 2007–February 3, 2008
The rise of abstraction eroded the tradition of figurative art in postwar America and Western Europe, except in areas cut off from the West. This exhibition presented works by a group of painters who, after the fall of the Berlin Wall in 1989, chose to study figurative painting at the centuries-old, conservative Leipzig Art Academy, located in what had been East Germany.

Angela Fraleigh, *all consequence as soon forgotten* (2005), in *Phantasmania* (2007)

2008

Nancy Hwang: This is not a couch.
February 1–29, 2008
For her site-specific project, Korean-born artist Nancy Hwang positioned herself in the Kemper Museum and engaged willing visitors in casual conversations, trying to facilitate relationships between individuals. Her work was designed to break down socially constructed barriers between people in public places.

You are one step closer to learning the truth
February 8–August 3, 2008
Deb Sokolow worked directly on the Kemper Museum's gallery walls, constructing elaborate diagrammatic drawings meant to read like a graphic novel with viewers assuming the role of the central character. The storyline followed an amateur detective's attempts to unravel a mystery.

Nancy Hwang: This is not a couch. (2008), installation view

Dan Christensen: Forty Years of Painting (2009), installation view

Biographical Landscape: The Photography of Stephen Shore, 1969–1979

February 22–May 18, 2008
This exhibition, organized by Aperture, showcased Stephen Shore's celebrated series *Uncommon Places*, documenting America of the late 1960s and early 1970s. More than 150 color-infused photographs presented the familiar—parking lots, apartment buildings, motel rooms, restaurants—with a striking sense of humanity.

Julia Oschatz: Where Else

April 4–July 6, 2008
German artist Julia Oschatz presented a room-size installation comprising paintings, drawings, and videos housed in cardboard constructions. Her looping videos blended performance, animation, and painted imagery, and charted the odyssey of a fictitious part-animal, part-human protagonist.

RubberMade: Sculptures by Chakaia Booker

June 6–August 17, 2008
Through a physically demanding process of twisting, slicing, and weaving found rubber tires (from bikes, cars, and farm equipment), Chakaia Booker formed dynamic, whimsical sculptures that fuse ecological concerns with questions about racial and economic differences, globalization, and sociopolitical power structures.

Anthony Lepore: Restoration

October 3, 2008–February 1, 2009
This exhibition of Anthony Lepore's revelatory color photographs examined relationships between humans and their environment. Lepore's subjects seemed to reveal a deep desire to restore their relationships with the people and places closest to them.

Jeff Shore and Jon Fisher: Reel to Reel

November 7, 2008–January 11, 2009
Fashioned from wood, wires, lights, motors, and automated video and audio components, *Reel to Reel* was a sculptural video installation that delivered a multisensory experience, advancing human interaction with new technologies. The exhibition was co-organized by the Kemper Museum and the Weatherspoon Art Museum, Greensboro, North Carolina.

Johanna Billing: Taking Turns
November 21, 2008–February 15, 2009
Swedish artist Johanna Billing's poignant videos and films addressed issues of individuality, isolation, public performance, and decisive action (or inaction) in the context of social engagements.

2009

Dan Christensen: Forty Years of Painting
May 15–August 30, 2009
This survey of paintings by the late Dan Christensen documented his never-ending quest to understand the possibilities of color, paint, and pictorial space. Though long associated with the Color Field movement, Christensen's relentless experimentation made him resistant to any one label or category while placing him among this country's most ambitious abstract and gestural painters.

Jaimie Warren: You Are So Beautiful in the Face
June 5–October 3, 2009
Through a pseudo-documentary lens, photographer Jaimie Warren captured the quirky personalities, places, and hilariously awkward moments shaping her everyday life. This was the artist's first solo museum exhibition.

Wyeth: Three Generations of Artistry
September 17–November 29, 2009
Together, the careers of N. C. Wyeth, Andrew Wyeth, and James Wyeth span more than one hundred years of American painting. This exhibition presented artwork by the Wyeth family, America's iconic art family, long associated with the people and the landscapes of Maine and Chadds Ford, Pennsylvania.

Keltie Ferris: Man Eaters
October 23, 2009–February 13, 2010
Keltie Ferris's methodically structured paintings evoked the digital networks and urban topographies of the twenty-first century. Ferris employed formalist strategies and materials—oil, acrylic, sprayed paint, and oil pastel—to create enigmatic and visually seductive abstractions.

N. C. Wyeth, *Octave Plunged* (1920), in *Wyeth: Three Generations of Artistry* (2009)

2010

Ian Davis: Faith in the Future
February 26–June 19, 2010
Ian Davis's paintings featured masses of men—all identically dressed—standing in ambiguous formations, leaving viewers to wonder whether the scenarios depict something that has just transpired or invite anticipation of an event yet to come. This was the artist's first solo museum exhibition.

David Bates: The Katrina Paintings
May 21–August 22, 2010
David Bates, like many Americans, was overwhelmed by 2005's Hurricane Katrina and its destruction of America's bucolic Gulf Coast. In *The Katrina Paintings*, the artist boldly addressed Katrina, one of the most severe and inexplicable tragedies of our time, and its devastating aftermath.

Acquisitions in Context: Marc Swanson
August 20, 2010–April 10, 2011
As part of the Kemper Museum's partnership with DST Systems, Inc., this exhibition focused on the work of Marc Swanson, including a commissioned sculptural homage to the American buffalo or bison, the majestic beast of the American West. The sculpture stands at the northeast corner of Ninth and Broadway in downtown Kansas City.

Gao Brothers: Grandeur and Catharsis
September 17, 2010–January 2, 2011
This exhibition showcased the work of China's Gao Brothers—Gao Qiang and Gao Zhen. In 1968 the artists' father was arrested as a counterrevolutionary and a few days later died while in custody. The Gao Brothers' works of art are at times politically charged, but in the end the brothers seek to forgive and understand China's complicated history.

Ana Maria Hernando: When the Women Sing
October 1, 2010–January 15, 2011
This Argentinian-born artist's work was inspired by her visits to a remote village in the mountains of Peru. The exhibition included works created from colorful Peruvian hand-crocheted petticoats, as well as cut-paper drawings inspired by the shape of flowers.

Ana Maria Hernando, *La Montaña Trae Barcas de Azucenas (The Mountain Brings Us Boats Full of Lilies), II* (2009), in *Ana Maria Hernando: When the Women Sing* (2010–11)

2011

Pattern ID

January 28–May 8, 2011
This exhibition, organized by the Akron Art Museum, Ohio, featured works by fifteen artists, including Mark Bradford, Lalla Essaydi, Yinka Shonibare, and Kehinde Wiley, who have turned to pattern and dress as a language with which to communicate who they are and where they originate, with the echoes of culture clash, immigration, and multiethnicity.

Video Villa: New Paintings by Barbara Grad

February 4–May 28, 2011
Barbara Grad's abstract paintings in this exhibition drew inspiration from the dynamic intersection of worlds seemingly at odds: maps found several years ago in a cache stored by her son, offering secret entrée into gaming worlds; and the aerial topography of the boundaries between the built and the natural world.

Eric Forstmann, *Amenia at 2:30 a.m.* (2010), in *Acquisitions in Context: Eric Forstmann* (2011)

Acquisitions in Context: Eric Forstmann

April 29–August 14, 2011
Eric Forstmann's painted images are reminiscent of Edward Hopper's works of isolation. This exhibition focused on his interiors of long-abandoned farmhouses and his nighttime scenes of the empty streets of Amenia, a small town in New York's Hudson Valley. *Amenia at 2:30 a.m.* (2010), commissioned by the Kemper Museum, was featured.

Pattern ID (2011), installation view

Revelation: Major Paintings by Jules Olitski (2011), installation view

Revelation: Major Paintings by Jules Olitski

May 20–August 28, 2011
This exhibition presented more than thirty significant works highlighting important periods and themes from Jules Olitski's career, from his early Stain Paintings of the 1960s to his Late Paintings. The exhibition—the first of Olitski's paintings since his death in 2007—traveled to the Museum of Fine Arts, Houston, Texas; the Toledo Museum of Art, Ohio; the American University Museum at the Katzen Arts Center, Washington, D.C., and the Baker Museum of Art, Naples, Florida.

Acquisitions in Context: June Ahrens

September 9–December 24, 2011
June Ahrens repurposed broken acrylic mirrors, broken jars, and bottles to address issues of loss, pain, fragility, danger, and survival. The shadows cast by these forms added another dimension to the installations and provided a way to integrate form and concept, going beyond language.

The Big Reveal

September 23, 2011–April 15, 2012
This exhibition highlighted more than thirty new acquisitions to the Permanent Collection including, as the focal point, the major installation *Untitled #1336 (Scalapino Nu Shu)* (2009–10) by Petah Coyne. This massive work features an apple tree and taxidermied pheasants and peacocks, among other nontraditional materials. New works by Jacob Collins, Red Grooms, Betty Woodman, and others were also featured.

Jeanne Quinn: Ceramic In(ter)ventions

October 7, 2011–January 7, 2012
This exhibition presented Jeanne Quinn's signature installations that combine porcelain in dynamic dialogue with

Jeanne Quinn, *A Thousand Tiny Deaths* (2009), in *Jeanne Quinn: Ceramic In(ter)ventions* (2011–12)

unexpected media, including paint, electricity, and balloons. The weight and balance of these inventive works joined a sense of fragility with the gravity of form.

2012

Wilbur Niewald: The Studio Portrait
January 13–September 23, 2012
While Wilbur Niewald has been best known for his Kansas City landscapes painted en plein air in the city's various parks, this exhibition focused on Niewald's portraits, painted in his studio beginning in the 1970s.

Eric Fertman: Here's Your Hat, What's Your Hurry?
February 3–July 28, 2012
This exhibition featured elaborate sculptures and drawings by Eric Fertman, created with the skillful hand of a woodworker and the collaged imagery of a cartoonist, and evoking works by Philip Guston and Constantin Brancusi.

Lois Dodd: Catching the Light
May 18–August 26, 2012
This was the first museum retrospective for New York- and Maine-based painter Lois Dodd. Featuring more than fifty paintings from six decades, the exhibition showcased the artist's cityscapes of New York and paintings of the woods and gardens of Maine. *Lois Dodd: Catching the Light* traveled to the Portland Museum of Art in Maine.

Be Inspired!
September 7, 2012–June 7, 2013
Be Inspired! connected works new to the Permanent Collection and the opportunity for the community to hear from the artists who created them. New work in diverse media by Nicole Awai, Angela Dufresne, Bo Joseph, Matt Rich, Jim Sajovic, and (non-Permanent Collection) filmmaker Stacey Steers was featured.

Eric Fertman: Here's Your Hat, What's Your Hurry? (2012), exterior installation view

The Map as Art
September 14, 2012–April 21, 2013
Inspired by the best-selling book *The Map as Art*, edited by Katharine "Kitty" Harmon, this exhibition presented works that explored issues of mapping—whether conceptually or literally—and the personal gesture involved in large-scale works. Works by Ingrid Calame, Nathan Carter, Tiffany Chung, Joyce Kozloff, Lordy Rodriguez, Robert Walden, and Heidi Whitman were featured.

2013

Laura McPhee: River of No Return
May 17–September 22, 2013
In her large-scale photographs—each measuring six by eight feet—Laura McPhee presented the landscape and culture of the American West with a special focus on the Sawtooth Valley in central Idaho, a desolate part of the United States. Her residency and the creation of the photographs were sponsored by the Alturas Foundation.

Laura McPhee: River of No Return (2013), installation view

Dressed Up (2013–14), installation view

Dressed Up
October 11, 2013–April 27, 2014
The theater of the self took center stage in *Dressed Up*, an exhibition of works in a range of media by artists Hope Gangloff, Trenton Doyle Hancock, Marcia Kure, and Neeta Madahar that defined the self-portrait as a conceptual view of the artist seen through their depictions of others who have a real or imagined connection to the artist.

Neeta Madahar: Falling
December 6, 2013–April 6, 2014
Neeta Madahar's video animation *Falling* (2005) mesmerized viewers with countless sycamore seeds cascading in slow motion, revealing the beauty and unexpected drama of our everyday surroundings. Accompanied by a musical score by composer Miguel d'Oliveira, *Falling* was jointly commissioned by Fabrica Photoworks and the Institute of International Visual Arts.

Acknowledgments

Museum co-founders Crosby and Bebe Kemper in front of Jules Olitski's *Prince Patutszky Pleasures* (1962), 2010

I t is with deep gratitude and profound respect that any acknowledgment must begin with the Museum's co-founder, R. Crosby Kemper Jr. His recent passing has brought into sharp relief the extraordinary passion and commitment to the cultural and civic life of Kansas City to which his life was dedicated. All that follows, both philosophically and in action, will stand in his shadow, while simultaneously shining a bright light on the possibilities of art impacting life. These seeming incongruous images reflect the unstoppable nature of Crosby and his unwavering belief in the beauty and power of art.

In 2012, after serving since 1995 as the Founding Chairman of the Board of Trustees of the Kemper Museum of Contemporary Art, R. Crosby Kemper Jr. retired from the Board. His wife and co-founder of the Museum, Mary "Bebe" Kemper, left the Board at that same time. Mary Kemper Wolf, their daughter, was named only the second Chairman of the Board in 2013. Her love of the Museum, her dedication to Kansas City, and her experience as a filmmaker and producer make her an ideal choice for this demanding role. Alexander "Sandy" Kemper and Mariner Kemper hold the other family positions, and currently filling out the Board of Trustees are Karen Holland, L. Joshua "Josh" Sosland, Jo Ann Sullivan, and Clyde Wendel, assisted by Board Secretary Dennis Rilinger. Founding Trustees Marilyn Bartlett Hebenstreit (retired in 2014) and Josh Sosland deserve special thanks for their long-standing guidance and leadership.

In 2011, the Board of Trustees made an important community outreach decision to form a Board of Directors, a group of Kansas Citians with a wide range of philanthropic and business experience. These

Directors, John Bluford, Bill Gautreaux, Tom Holcom, and Lindsay Major, attend all meetings of the Board of Trustees and have become a trusted and valued advisory council. The diversity of voices they offer has indeed been of great service to the Kemper Museum.

In August 2012, longtime Museum supporters Stanley Bushman and Charles Helzberg presented a challenge to the members of National Committee, our highest level of membership. With an extraordinary gift, they set in motion the 20th Anniversary Appeal, with the intent of meeting a million-dollar goal. A wide range of Museum supporters responded to this appeal,

(standing left to right): Board Secretary Dennis Rilinger; Museum Directors and Trustees Tom Holcom, Lindsay Major, Karen Holland, Jo Ann Sullivan, Marilyn Bartlett Hebenstreit, Bill Gautreaux, John Bluford; (seated left to right): Josh Sosland, Mary Kemper Wolf, Bebe Kemper, R. Crosby Kemper Jr., Clyde Wendel, (not pictured): Sandy Kemper, Mariner Kemper, 2012

giving both financial gifts and works of art by Andrew Wyeth, Petah Coyne, Ed Blackburn, and Barry Anderson, among many others, adding depth to the Permanent Collection. It is to our visitors, members, and the Kansas City community that we owe great thanks for supporting, with their visits and donations, the goals of the Kemper Museum: to collect, care for, and interpret the art of our time and to bring art to life for every visitor.

Of course, none of this important work could be accomplished without a talented and dedicated staff—a team I am honored to lead. Some, like Docent Educator Tara Andris, joined the Kemper staff just this year; others, like Executive Chef Jennifer Maloney, have become as much a part of the Museum culture as the Dale Chihuly permanent installations in the atrium. I joined the Kemper Museum in fall 2009 as Curator. Returning to my Midwest roots to support the goals of the Kemper has been a marvelous opportunity. In June 2012, I was named Executive Director of the Museum, a privilege for which I am deeply grateful.

The publication you are holding is impressive evidence of the Kemper Museum team spirit. Michelle Bolton King served as our project manager who with tact and grace kept us all focused on the final product; Margaret A. Keough, former director of marketing and communications, oversaw all aspects of this project with her rare and invaluable combination of humor, insight, and the highest degree of professionalism. Claudia Marchand, who has for the past several years produced our Museum printed matter, designed this elegant catalogue. Acting Museum Registrar Elizabeth Lumpkin and Curator and Head of Adult Public Programs Erin Dziedzic were essential to the research and careful oversight that a project of this magnitude requires. Collections Manager and Registrar Andrea Phillips secured timely details and helped usher the project to successful completion.

Overseeing both the "front" and "back" of house at the Kemper Museum is akin to creating an inviting theatrical experience for our visitors. Steve Crays, Museum protection manager, trains the friendly first faces that visitors see upon entering any of our three locations. Museum protection officers, like all of our staff, take seriously their role as representatives of this esteemed institution. Senior Museum protection staff include Neal Dazey and Kemper East Site Supervisor Christain Hartman. The Museum properties are kept in sparkling order by Paul Watts, facility and operations manager, and the many grounds and maintenance crew members that he supervises.

The art on view, both from the Permanent Collection and in exhibitions organized by the Museum, is evidence of the fine work of a team that includes Erin Dziedzic; Elizabeth Lumpkin; Andrea Phillips; and Russ Horton, head preparator and exhibition designer. They are assisted by additional staff, interns, and volunteers to make the complexities of caring for the Permanent Collection and designing, installing, and lighting exhibitions appear effortless. The visitor experience is dynamically enriched by the fine work of Children and Family Museum Educator Brenda Brinkhous-Hatch and Docent Educator and Volunteer Coordinator Tara Andris.

Behind the scenes are dedicated senior staff who make our daily operations run smoothly. Kathy Surber, director of finance and accounting, is my partner in having a clear-eyed, always-current assessment of the Museum's needs and ability to reach our shared goals. Kathy is ably assisted by Kathleen Fisher and Melanie Middlebrook. Don Schreiner, director of development, heads a department that builds and maintains important relationships with our members and donor community while creating our signature annual events—National Committee weekend and our Gala. Betty Kindler, special events coordinator, and Sara Hale, development and membership coordinator, are essential talents and support our institutional stability.

The amenities offered by the Kemper Museum are without parallel. Staff responsible for this enhanced visitor experience include Café Sebastienne's Executive Chef Jennifer Maloney, General Manager Keith Goldman, and their entire kitchen and wait staff. Café Manager Tina Block and Assistant Manager Sloane Harper along with Sous Chef Janet Ross are central to the Café's easy elegance. Museum Shop Manager Raina Heinrich and the retail associates offer some of the finest handcrafted jewelry and clothing along with books and cards related to each changing exhibition.

There are too many other staff to list individually, but they each have my respect and appreciation for the professional experience, creativity, and collegial attitude they bring to work each and every day. With the leadership of the Trustees, the continued support of our donors and visitors, and the determined work of Museum staff, I trust that the next twenty years will be filled with meaningful contributions to Kansas City, the region, and the contemporary art world. On behalf of the entire Kemper community, please allow me to express a profound pride in the history and an abiding faith in the future of the Kemper Museum of Contemporary Art.

Barbara O'Brien
Executive Director
Kemper Museum of Contemporary Art

Kemper Museum of Contemporary Art
20th Anniversary Donors

With gratitude, we thank the donors who gave in response to our 20th Anniversary Appeal, a three-year initiative, and those who gave gifts in honor or memory of Mr. R. Crosby Kemper Jr., August 29, 2012, through January 21, 2014.

June and Ron Ahrens
Don and Christine Alexander
I. Allis
Laura A. Anderson
Anonymous Donor
Atrium Gallery, Carolyn and Joseph Miles
Atterbury Family Foundation
Bartlett & Co. Grain Charitable Foundation
Paul and Joan Bartlett
Cynthia and Warner Baxter
Linda and Tom Beal
Judy and Fred Bellemere
Charles and Jeanne Bleakley
Blish-Mize Co.
Mary and Tom Bloch
Kenneth and Lisa Block
Joanne and John Bluford
Suzy and David Bradley
Mary Shaw Branton
Jeanne and Scott Brown
Nancy and Timothy Buese
Stanley J. Bushman and Ann Canfield
Byron Cohen Gallery
Carol Swanson Price Foundation
Central Power Systems & Services, Inc.
Charles D. Williams & Co.
Susan and John Clarke
Elizabeth and Stephen Clarke
Ken Cohen
Community National Bank & Trust
Brenda and William Conner
Debby and Gary Cortes
Chris and Claudia Curtiss

Sandi and David De Walt and family
Shirley A. De Walt
Terry and Peggy Dunn
E. M. Lynn Foundation
Sandra Eveloff
Peggy Farney
Eric Fertman
Fogel-Anderson Construction Co.
Frank Fowler
J. Scott Francis
Caroline French
Norm Fretwell and Bev Haskins
Bill and Christy Gautreaux
Clare and Pete Genovese
Courtney Goddard-Hawkinson
   and Dana Hawkinson
Deanna and Greg Graves
Margaret Gustin
Lona and Robert Hansen
Harry Portman Charitable Trust
Larry Hawk
Marilyn and Jim Hebenstreit
Shirley and Barnett Helzberg
Charles M. Helzberg and Sandra Baer
Paget and Tom Higgins
Tom and Denise Holcom
Joan Horan
Hufft Projects
Jack and Barbara Hughes
Dr. and Mrs. John Hunkeler
Susan Inglett
Ireland Stapleton Pryor & Pascoe, PC
JMW & Associates, LLC

Linda and Topper Johntz
Richard F. Jones
Roberto Juarez and David Freberg
Rick Kahle
Richard and Martha Katz
KCP&L
Linda Coburn Kornitzer and Bill Kornitzer
James W. Lacy and Sherry Cromwell-Lacy
Sanders Lambert Jr.
Lynn Adkins and Linda Lighton
Mike and Linda Lyon
Bill and Peggy Lyons
Lindsay H. Major
Steve and Mary Lynn Marks
Barbara Hall Marshall
The McDonnell Foundation, Inc.
McNational, Inc.
Medart, Inc.
Mid-America Arts Alliance
Nancy Milgram
Miller Haviland Ketter PC, PA
Darlia and David Morris
Rozzie and Will Motter
Jeff Mullen
Muriel McBrien Kauffman Foundation
Margaret and Jerome Nerman
NIC Inc.
Jeannette Nichols
Mr. and Mrs. Richard Orr
Cynthia and Dale Parker and family
Parris Communication / Roshann Parris
    and Jeff Dobbs
Gwenna and John Pence
Jeanne Quinn
Palle and Dennis Rilinger
Randy and Sandy Rolf
Ann and Alan Rolley
Kathy and Tom Sanders
Betty and Tom Scott
Charles Sharpe
Myra and Lester Siegel Jr.
Sosland Foundation
Joshua and Jane Sosland
Morton and Estelle Sosland

Sprint
Jo Ann and William Sullivan
Marvin Szneler
Mr. and Mrs. Wayne Thiebaud
Ruthie and Harold Tivol
Timothy Travis
Elizabeth and Paul Uhlmann III
Universal Engraving, Inc.
Jane Voorhees
Warren Weaver
Katie and Clyde Wendel
Steve Werner
Sally and Robert West
Toma and Andy Wolff
Patty and Tom Wood
Thomas and Sally Wood Family Foundation

Donors of Works of Art to the Permanent Collection in Honor of the Museum's 20th Anniversary

June Ahrens
Barry Anderson
Anonymous
Linda and Ed Blackburn
Christopher Brown
    and John Berggruen Gallery
Chihuly Studio
Frauke de Looper and Atrium Gallery
Lois Dodd and Alexandre Gallery
Angela Dufresne
Barbara Grad
Ana Maria Hernando and Robischon Gallery
Roberto Juarez and Shark's Ink.
Don Lambert and Lawrence Art Center
Lawrence Lithography Workshop
Hung Liu and Jeff Kelly
Dean Mitchell
Lolly and Jim Mitchell
Gerry and Wilbur Niewald
Matt Rich and Samsøñ, Boston
Lee and Nicholas Wyeth

Selected Works of Art Donated in Honor of
the Museum's 20th Anniversary

Dale Chihuly, *Chandelier Drawing*, 2013
acrylic on paper
30 x 22 inches
Gift of Chihuly Studio in honor of the 20th Anniversary
of the Kemper Museum of Contemporary Art, 2013.13

Petah Coyne, *Untitled (#887P-97)*, 1997
gelatin silver print, edition 1/7
60 x 40 inches
Anonymous gift in honor of Bebe and Crosby Kemper
on the occasion of the 20th Anniversary of the
Kemper Museum of Contemporary Art, 2013.15

Lois Dodd, *Hydrangea*, 1997
oil on Masonite
12 x 18 inches
Gift of the artist and Alexandre Fine Art, NY in honor of the
20th Anniversary of the Kemper Museum of Contemporary Art, 2014.3

Ana Maria Hernando, *Nuestra Canción Anaranjada*
(Our Orange Song), 2012
acrylic ink and acrylic on paper
41½ x 30 inches
Gift of Ana Maria Hernando and Robischon Gallery in honor of the
20th Anniversary of the Kemper Museum of Contemporary Art, 2013.26

Dean Mitchell, *Working Woman*, 2013
watercolor on paper
8¼ x 8⅞ inches
Gift of the artist in honor of the 20th Anniversary of
the Kemper Museum of Contemporary Art, 2013.11

Matt Rich, *Blue*, 2014
gouache on Arches paper
13 x 10 inches
Gift of the artist and Samsøñ, Boston, Massachusetts, in honor of
the 20th Anniversary of the Kemper Museum of Contemporary Art, 2014.7

Andrew Wyeth, *Wolf River Apples (study)*, 1959
watercolor and pencil on paper
13½ x 10⅞ inches
Gift of Lee and Nicholas Wyeth in honor of Crosby Kemper
on the occasion of the 20th Anniversary of the Kemper Museum
of Contemporary Art, 2013.14

Credits

All photographs © and courtesy of the Kemper Museum of Contemporary Art unless otherwise noted.

cover: Petah Coyne, *Untitled #827 (Three Tiered Chandelier)* (detail), 1996 (see p. 55). Art © Petah Coyne, Courtesy Galerie Lelong, New York. Photograph: Courtesy James Allison Photography, 2013

p. 4: June Ahrens, *Hiding in Plain Site*, 2011, in *Acquisitions in Context: June Ahrens*, 2011. Art © June Ahrens. Photograph: Bruce Mathews

p. 7: Photograph: Tammy Wainwright

p. 8: Louise Bourgeois, *Spider*, 1996, cast 1997 (see p. 40, bottom). Art © The Easton Foundation/Licensed by VAGA, New York, NY. Photograph: Dan Wayne

p. 9 (top): Tom Otterness, *Crying Giant*, 2002 (see p. 127). Art © Tom Otterness/tomotterness.net

p. 9 (bottom): Jules Olitski, *Eos the Titan*, 2006 (see p. 125, bottom). Art © Estate of Jules Olitski/Licensed by VAGA New York, NY

p. 10: Childe Hassam, *Nude, Appledore, Isle of Shoals*, 1913 (see p. 77). Photograph: Courtesy Gerald Peters Gallery

p. 11 (top): © David Bates, Collection of the Ogden Museum of Southern Art, Gift of the artist. Photograph: Bruce Mathews

p. 11 (bottom): Archie Scott Gobber, *In Loving Memory of You*, 2008 (see p. 69). Art © Archie Scott Gobber, Courtesy Haw Contemporary, Kansas City, Missouri.

p. 12 (top): Jeff Shore | Jon Fisher, *Reel to Reel*, 2007; wood, aluminum, Plexiglas, electric motors, LED lights, light bulbs, wire, miniature surveillance cameras, custom electronics, felt, plastic, guitar strings, effects modules, tuning machine heads, vinyl records, record player stylus, video projector, computers, audio mixer, audio amplifier, speakers, video fader, dimensions variable, duration 8 mins. Art © Jeff Shore and Jon Fisher. Photograph: Bruce Mathews

p. 12 (bottom): Photograph: Mark McDonald

p. 13 (bottom): Photograph: Tammy Wainwright

p. 14: Art © The Gao Brothers. Photograph: Bruce Mathews

p. 15 (bottom): Photograph: Bruce Mathews

pp. 16–17: *Gao Brothers: Grandeur and Catharsis*, 2010–11, installation view. Art © The Gao Brothers. Photograph: Bruce Mathews

pp. 18–19: Jules Olitski, *Eos the Titan*, 2006 (see p. 125, bottom). Art © Estate of Jules Olitski/Licensed by VAGA New York, NY. Photograph: Courtesy James Allison Photography, 2013

pp. 20–21: Jeanne Quinn, *Everything Is Not As It Seems*, 2009, in *Jeanne Quinn: Ceramic In(ter)ventions*, 2011–12. Art © Jeanne Quinn, Courtesy of the artist. Photograph: Bruce Mathews

p. 25: Art © Magdalena Abakanowicz, Courtesy Marlborough Gallery, New York

p. 26 (top): Art © 2014 The Josef and Anni Albers Foundation. Photograph: Dan Wayne

p. 26 (bottom): Art © Jose Alvarez (D.O.P.A.). Photograph Courtesy Marlborough Gallery, New York

p. 27: Art and Photographs © Barry Anderson

p. 28: Art © 2004 Polly Apfelbaum

p. 29 (top): Art © The Archipenko Foundation / Artists Rights Society (ARS), New York

p. 29 (bottom): Art © Estate of Robert Arneson/Licensed by VAGA, New York, NY

p. 30 (top): Art © Nicole Awai

p. 30 (bottom): Art © Nicole Awai. Photograph: Courtesy James Allison Photography, 2013

p. 31: Art © The Estate of Francis Bacon. All rights reserved. / DACS, London / ARS, NY 2014. Photograph: Courtesy James Allison Photography, 2013

p. 32 (top, detail): Art © David Bates. Photograph: David Wharton

p. 32 (bottom): Art © David Bates. Photograph: Courtesy the artist

p. 33: Art © Romare Bearden Foundation/Licensed by VAGA, New York, NY. Photographs: Courtesy James Allison Photography, 2013

p. 34: Art © T.H. Benton and R.P. Benton Testamentary Trusts/UMB Bank Trustee/Licensed by VAGA, New York, NY. Photograph: Courtesy Gerald Peters Gallery

p. 35: Art © Robin Bernat. Photograph: Bruce Mathews

p. 36: Art © Ed Blackburn. Photograph: Courtesy James Allison Photography, 2013

p. 37: Art and Photographs © Julie Blackmon

p. 38: Art © 2014 Christian Boltanski / Artists Rights Society (ARS), New York / ADAGP, Paris. Photograph Courtesy Marian Goodman Gallery

p. 39: Art © Chakaia Booker

p. 40 (top): Art © Fernando Botero, Courtesy Marlborough Gallery, New York. Photograph: Courtesy James Allison Photography, 2013

p. 40 (bottom): Art © The Easton Foundation/Licensed by VAGA, New York, NY. Photograph: Dan Wayne

p. 41 (top): Art © Christopher Brown, Courtesy John Berggruen Gallery. Photograph: Dan Wayne

p. 41 (bottom left and right): Art and Photographs © Christopher Brown, Courtesy John Berggruen Gallery

p. 42: Art © Frederick J. Brown Trust. Photographs: Courtesy James Allison Photography, 2013

p. 43: Art © Frederick J. Brown Trust. Photograph: Dan Wayne

p. 44: Art © Deborah Butterfield/Licensed by VAGA, New York, NY. Photograph: Courtesy James Allison Photography, 2013

p. 45: Art © Ingrid Calame. Photograph: Courtesy James Allison Photography, 2013

p. 46 (top): Art © The Estate of Harry Callahan, Courtesy Pace/MacGill Gallery, New York. Photograph: Dan Wayne

p. 46 (bottom) Art and Photograph © The Estate of Harry Callahan, Courtesy Pace/MacGill Gallery, New York

p. 47: Art © Suzanne Caporael. Photographs: Courtesy James Allison Photography, 2013

p. 48 (top): Art © Squeak Carnwath/Licensed by VAGA, New York, NY. Photograph: Courtesy James Allison Photography, 2013

p. 48 (bottom): Art © Brendan Cass, Courtesy the artist and McClain Gallery, Houston, TX

p. 49: Art © 2014 Fairweather & Fairweather LTD / Artists Rights Society (ARS), New York. Photograph: Courtesy of the artist and Gagosian Gallery

p. 50–51: Art © Dale Chihuly. Photographs: Dan Wayne

p. 52: Art © Estate of Daniel J. Christensen/Licensed by VAGA, New York, NY. Photographs: Dan Wayne

p. 53 (top): Art © Jacob Collins, Courtesy of the artist and Adelson Galleries

p. 53 (bottom): Art and Photograph © The Joseph and Robert Cornell Memorial Foundation/ Licensed by VAGA, New York, NY

p. 54 (top): Art © Petah Coyne, Courtesy Galerie Lelong, New York. Photograph: Mark McDonald

p. 54 (bottom): Photograph: Tammy Wainwright

p. 55: Art © Petah Coyne, Courtesy Galerie Lelong, New York. Photographs: Courtesy James Allison Photography, 2013

p. 56 (top): Art © 2014 The Willem de Kooning Foundation / Artists Rights Society (ARS), New York. Photograph: Courtesy James Allison Photography, 2013

p. 178: Teresa Hubbard/Alexander Birchler, still from *House with Pool*, 2004; video installation, dimensions variable. Art and Photograph © the artists and Tanya Bondakar Gallery, New York

p. 179: Photograph: Bruce Mathews

p. 180 (top): Anne Lindberg, *democracy*, 2005; wooden table, wire words, 135 x 30 x 23 inches, transcription of "Commencement" by Terry Tempest Williams, from *The Open Space of Democracy*. Art © Anne Lindberg. Photograph: Derek Porter

p. 180 (bottom): Marcie Miller Gross, *Intersection*, 2005; cotton huck towels, dimensions variable. Art © Marcie Miller Gross. Photograph: E. G. Schempf

p. 181: Lisa Sanditz, *Oklahoma City on New Year's Eve*, 2005; acrylic on canvas, 30 x 40 inches, Collection of Kenneth and Nancy Kranzberg, St. Louis, MO. Art and Photograph © Lisa Sanditz, Courtesy the artist and CRG Gallery, NY, and Ken and Nancy Kranzberg

p. 182 (top): Jennifer Steinkamp, *The Wreck of the Dumaru*, 2004; video installation, dimensions variable. Art © Jennifer Steinkamp, Courtesy the artist and Lehmann Maupin, New York and Hong Kong. Photograph: Bruce Mathews

p. 182 (bottom): Angela Fraleigh, *all consequence as soon forgotten*, 2005; oil and alkyd resin on canvas, 99⅜ x 141¼ inches, Museum purchase made possible by a gift from Dr. Michael Bastasch in honor of Kathleen A. and Paul M. Bastasch and Elizabeth Dunbar, 2007.6. Art © Angela Fraleigh. Photograph: Thomas R. DuBrock

p. 183: Nancy Hwang, *This is not a couch.*, 2008. Art © Nancy Hwang

p. 184: Art © Estate of Daniel J. Christensen/Licensed by VAGA, New York, NY. Photograph: Bruce Mathews

p. 185: N. C. Wyeth, *Octave Plunged*, 1920; oil on canvas, 36 x 25 inches, Courtesy of Adelson Galleries, Frank E. Fowler and Somerville Manning Gallery. Photograph: © John Bigelow Taylor

p. 186: Ana Maria Hernando, *La Montaña Trae Barcas de Azucenas (The Mountain Brings Us Boats Full of Lilies), II*, 2009; petticoats, beads, embroidered flowers in polymer resin, dimensions variable. Art © Ana Maria Hernado, Courtesy Robischon Gallery. Photograph: Bruce Mathews

p. 187 (top): Eric Forstmann, *Amenia at 2:30 a.m.*, 2010; oil on board, 25 x 48 inches, Museum purchase made possible by a gift from the Kearney Wornall Foundation, 2011.11. Art © Eric Forstmann, Courtesy Eckert Fine Art. Photograph: Bruce Mathews

p. 187 (bottom): (left) Yinka Shonibare MBE, *La Méduse*, 2008; chromogenic print on aluminum, Collection of Akron Art Museum, Akron, OH; (center) Yinka Shonibare MBE, *Three Graces*, 2001; fiberglass mannequins, Dutch wax printed cotton. Art © 2014 Artists Rights Society (ARS), New York / DACS, London; (right) Kehinde Wiley, *Santos Dumont—The Father of Aviation III*, 2009; oil on canvas, Private collection, Courtesy of Roberts & Tilton, Culver City, CA. Art © Kehinde Wiley. Photograph: Bruce Mathews

p. 188 (top): Art © Estate of Jules Olitski/Licensed by VAGA, New York, NY. Photograph: Dan Wayne

p. 188 (bottom): Jeanne Quinn, *A Thousand Tiny Deaths*, 2009. Art © Jeanne Quinn. Photograph: Bruce Mathews

p. 189: Art © Eric Fertman, Courtesy Susan Inglett Gallery. Photograph: Bruce Mathews

p. 190: Art © Laura McPhee, Collection of Alturas Foundation and Courtesy of Carroll and Sons. Photograph: Bruce Mathews

p. 191: (left) Marcia Kure, *Dressed Up #3*, 2010. Art © Marcia Kure, Courtesy Susan Inglett Gallery and Johannes Lehmann; (center) Marcia Kure, *Dressed Up #6*, 2010. Art © Marcia Kure, Courtesy Susan Inglett Gallery and Sherman Edmiston III; (right) Hope Gangloff, *Olga*, 2012. Art © Hope Gangloff, Courtesy Susan Inglett Gallery and private collector. Photograph: Tammy Wainwright

p. 192: Jules Olitski, *Prince Patutszky Pleasures*, 1962 (see p. 125, top). Art © Estate of Jules Olitski/Licensed by VAGA New York, NY. Photograph: Dan Wayne

p. 193: Photograph: Mark McDonald

p. 198: Art © Dale Chihuly. Photograph: Courtesy Chihuly Studio

p. 199: Art and Photograph © Petah Coyne, Courtesy Galerie Lelong, New York

p. 200: Art and Photograph © Lois Dodd/Licensed by VAGA, New York, NY. Courtesy of Alexandre Gallery, New York

p. 201: Art © Ana Maria Hernando. Photograph: Ken Sanville

p. 202: Art © Dean Mitchell. Photograph: Courtesy James Allison Photography, 2013

p. 203: Art © Matt Rich, Courtesy the artist and Samsøñ, Boston, Massachusetts. Photograph Courtesy the artist

p. 204: Art © Andrew Wyeth. Photograph: Courtesy James Allison Photography, 2013

Marking 20 Years: Kemper Museum of Contemporary Art is published on the occasion of the 20th anniversary of the Kemper Museum of Contemporary Art, Kansas City, Missouri.

Kemper Museum of Contemporary Art
4420 Warwick Boulevard
Kansas City, MO 64111
www.kemperart.org

Library of Congress Control Number: 2014900271
ISBN 978-1-891246-25-8

Edited by Michelle Bolton King
Designed by Claudia Marchand
Printed by J. S. McCarthy, Augusta, ME
Bound by HFGroup/Acme Bookbinding, Charlestown, MA
Typeset in Pluto®, Pluto Sans®, Yalta Sans®, © and licensed by Linotype GmbG